SUBORDINATION
and
DEVELOPMENT

Emerging Market Economies
of Asia and Latin America

Sunanda Sen

 Tulika Books

The global interdependence of economies through international markets is historically associated with the exploitation of differences and the generation of asymmetries. Sunanda Sen's book highlights the role of expanding markets in triggering cumulative processes of subordination of certain economies (or groups of economies) relative to others. This book is an invaluable contribution to understanding the complex trajectories along which patterns of subordination are currently challenged and transformed.

ROBERTO SCAZZIERI
Italian National Lincei Academy and
University of Bologna

Subordination and Development is an outstanding study of our current phase of capitalist development, brilliantly characterized as a modern blend of financialization and neo-imperialism. Using a highly informative analytical economic framework, based on Keynes's and post-Keynesian contributions, the book shows how the global South is caught in a web of unequal financial and trade relationships with the global North. The book is truly enlightening and compelling because Professor Sen applies her analytical framework to case studies of Argentina, Brazil, Mexico, India and China. These studies show the financialized subordination in practice and their highly negative impacts on these Southern countries. I highly recommend the book to all those interested in understanding the underlying dynamics of finance and unequal development in today's world.

GERALD EPSTEIN
Professor of Economics and Co-Director,
Political Economy Research Institute (PERI),
University of Massachusetts Amherst

Sunanda Sen successfully interweaves Gramscian concepts of hegemony and subordination with Marxian ideas of fictitious capital to analyse the nexus between corporates, finance, the state, and global regulatory and finance institutions, as they coalesce into an embryonic global elite. This domination by 'new capital' involves the detachment of finance from the real economy, with money chasing its own tail for artificial profits in the global South. Combining perspectives drawn from heterodox theoretical traditions with applied statistical analysis, this pioneering, innovative and erudite exploration illuminates key contemporary economic policy issues dominating national and international discourse. A very valuable contribution that will surely catalyse much creative investigation; strongly recommended for researchers, policy makers, teachers and advanced students in the wide-ranging fields of finance and development.

ASHWANI SAITH
Emeritus Professor, Institute of Social Studies, The Hague

Published by
Tulika Books
86/1 (ground floor), Shahpur Jat, New Delhi 110 049, India
www.tfortulika.com

First edition (hardback) 2025

ISBN: 978-81-965803-0-8

Printed at Chaman Enterprises, Delhi 110 002

With fond remembrance of
AMIYA K. BAGCHI
(1936–2024)

Contents

List of Figures

CHAPTER 4 Subordinating Financialization in Emerging Market Economies (EMEs) of Asia

Preface

An idea of 'subordination' and its related implications in the developing countries has been with the present author over some time. Subordination, as she could observe by looking around, relates to the power of the advanced economies to incapacitate the weaker nations from initiating domestic economic policies which could be of benefit to their own economies.

As it happens, the churning of ideas continued, next leading to a set of questions which sought some explanations for the ongoing compulsion or indoctrination on the part of the developing countries in their implementing policies advanced from abroad, having deleterious consequences in their domestic economies. For the advanced countries the outcome of the same set of policies was naturally beneficial.

Probing further, a clue could be found in the supremacy of the liberalized market, to have the capacity to operate as a self-appointed agent of corporate capital and multinational institutions abroad (the Bretton Woods institutions), and to make sure that policies followed by the developing countries do not deviate from those advanced from abroad, in general subscribing to neoliberal economics. The goal of the liberalized market has been to make it possible for overseas corporates to maximize the appropriation and enable the transfers of surpluses from the developing countries. The market also sets up reprisals against official policies in developing economies for their slightest deviations from the neoliberal prescriptions to liberalize capital markets. The consequence is often a reversal of capital flows away of the capital-importing economies. The twin manoeuvres, of implementing neoliberal policies and their continuation with threats of reprisals, have thus been continuing across countries, despite their retrograde effects on the developing countries.

The present study, while researched over years without any institutional support, had the benefit of immense support from friends, including former colleagues and students, from all over. The study could not have been completed without the help I received from so many of them, including Amiya Bagchi, Anjan Chakrabarty, Byasdeb Dasgupta, C.P. Chandrasekhar, Cristina Marcuzzo, Gary Dymski, Gerald Epstein, Ivano Cardinale, Jayati Ghosh, John Eatwell, L.P. Rochon, Lorain Kennedy, Paolo Paesani, Pierre Salama, Prabhat Patnaik, Roberto Scazzieri and Tetsuji Kawamura.

A special mention with thanks is deserved by the young researcher Nilanjan Ghosh who was behind processing all the official statistics used in the book.

I also mention here the immense support provided by Indira Chandrasekhar of Tulika Books in providing the editorial inputs which made the publication possible. I remain grateful to her for the help.

Finally, it remains to mention Sunrita (Mishtu) and Vipul for providing logistical support, much needed all through the long period I was preoccupied with writing the book! I remain grateful for their support, sharing the moments of crisis as well as of happiness!

Delhi, August 2025   SUNANDA SEN

1

A Prelude

The title as well as the contents of this book demand an explanation. It deviates from the studies that are available on emerging market economies (EMEs), by treating them as just a separate category of developing countries. Our analysis probes into the subordinate status of the EMEs, while relying on an attempt to highlight the general pattern of the ongoing subordination and the related lack of autonomy in framing their domestic economic policies as experienced by those economies. The reason underlying our selection of three EMEs from Latin America and two from Asia for anlaysis is as follows: for the Latin American countries, namely Brazil, Argentina and Mexico, the early initiation of liberalized financial flows from overseas; and for the two chosen from Asia, the fact that they are undisputedly high-growth economies in the world. The Asian EMEs include China, which happens to be the recipient of the highest flows of overseas finance reaching the developing countries in recent times; and India, which too receives significant flows of overseas finance as compared to other developing economies in South Asia.

SUBORDINATION AND LOSS OF AUTONOMY

The loss of autonomy in fixing domestic economic policies is not new for the developing countries, including those described as EMEs. The pattern of their current subordination replicates what was common in the past to the formal colonies of imperialist nations, or to countries that continued as neo-colonies in the recent post-war years. But there is a difference: while the prevailing lack of autonomy bears a semblance to the colonial era with transfers of surpluses/resources abroad, the earlier period also saw a formal political subservience of the colony to the ruling nation. This is different in the current pattern of subordination where the free market has surfaced as the primary agent to arrange the transfers of surpluses, as well as to continue the surveillance of overseas capital and the state over the ongoing economic policies in the subservient countries. In effect, the policies followed in those countries, despite their political independence, reflect a state of economic subordination with a lack of autonomy to decide on policies that suit their economies.

In the majority of developing economies, there prevailed an interregnum between the period marked by colonial rule and the more recent phase, when command over policymaking was transmitted by the free market operating as an agency of big capital and the state overseas. In between there were years when policies in the capital-receiving countries came from the donor governments as well as the multilateral agencies offering official aid. It was a period, as we will dwell on later, that can be identified as an *era of dependence* for aid-receiving countries in the global South. The pattern as above, described as *dependencia*, was distinctly different from what has followed since the mid-1990s, with global integration under the informal reign of liberalized markets under globalization in the neo-colonies. The latter were largely regimented to serve the large corporations originating from the advanced economies. The change marked the initiation of subordination, which transformed the economic policies of those countries by making them consistent with the interests of large capital held by the corporates in the advanced nations. The change that was brought in also implied a complete switch-over to neoliberal policies which have their base in mainstream economic theory. This was because of the explicit preference for and faith in neoliberal economics by the donor organizations on the part of the overseas state, and their transmission to the host economies by using the market. The market in turn was empowered with the capacity to stall any deviations of policies from ongoing neoliberal norms as prescribed by the donors. This was accomplished by reprisals which often initiated reversals of the ongoing capital inflows or a drop in the international credit-rating as estimated by the rating agencies. Signals were carried forward by the market with changes, say, in the reduced capital inflows. Similar processes in the EMEs, as documented in the following chapters, can be identified as a process of 'subordination' in those countries, specifically identified with their loss of autonomy over economic policies implemented in their own country.

INTEGRATION OF MARKETS UNDER GLOBALIZATION

For developing countries, integration with the rest of world under globalization came with a steady opening up of their markets. Simultaneously there arose a set of new relations between the developing and the advanced countries which remained grossly unequal. The process transformed the majority of countries in the periphery into neo-colonies with a binding obligation to accept the compulsive diktats of the market in favour of big capital located in the advanced economies.

THE STRUCTURE OF THE BOOK

The book consists of five chapters including the present one. Chapter 2 provides, first, a critical analysis of the theoretical frame of neoliberal economics, used to provide the oft-used manuals for the financial markets of most developing and emerging market economies (EMEs). The next two chapters, 3 and 4, on the EMEs, bring out the details of the implementation and the deleterious consequences of such policies for those economies.

We have relied, in our critique of the neoliberal approach from a heterodox point of view, on the Keynesian tradition. It includes Keynes' questioning in his book, *A Treatise on Probability* (1921), of the Benthamite utilitarian calculations of probability on the basis of frequency of events; later disputed further in Keynes' magnum opus, *The General Theory* (1936). By then Keynes' analysis, encountering the context of uncertainty, was using a 'subjective' approach to probability, interpreting the ongoing tendency of 'animal spirits' prevailing in liberalized markets. The formulation on uncertainty has been at centre stage in the writings of the Post-Keynesians which followed.

Analysis of the conceptual problems of neoliberal economic policies and their harmful consequences in the real economy of countries provide the backdrop for the need to use alternate approaches and policies in the heterodox tradition. As a background we provide, in chapter 2, some heterodox explanations of the ongoing stagnation, which are relevant in the context of the EMEs we are dealing with.

Chapter 2 then proceeds to discuss some related issues in the Post-Keynesian literature, in particular the emergence of financialization that was witnessed in different countries with the prices of short-term and uncertain financial assets rising relative to the prices of assets on long-term real transactions. The large demand in favour of short-term financial assets moving up their prices can be linked to the booming inflows of short-term capital under deregulation, as can be noticed in the EMEs we have studied in the chapters which follow.

Dealing with the origin of financialization at a conceptual level, chapter 2 refers to what Keynes formulated as the 'finance motive' of holding liquidity for purchasing short-term financial assets like equities in his *Quarterly Journal of Economics* article of 1937.[1] Thus, in terms of the 'finance motive', the liquidity demand for holding short-term financial assets is essentially linked to investments which are based on speculation.

Chapter 2 also includes an account of how finance could achieve a state of *dominance* in most economies under deregulated financial flows. The pattern of structural dynamics in those economies includes a steady increase in the share of the services sector to aggregate output (GDP at constant prices), which of late has been 50 per cent or more of GDP in both the advanced and the developing countries. The pattern has prevailed particularly since the onset of the recession during the global financial crisis of 2007–08, which resulted in a downswing of industrial activities – both in absolute terms and as a share of the GDP. As for the composition of the services sector, high-value and speculative financial transactions have emerged as the major activity in terms of their value added as services. As with the large ratio of the aggregate value of services to GDP, finance contributes a similar share to the GDP which has also been large. The similarity offers an explanation of the growing power and dominance of finance which is supported by its *quantitative* significance as above in economies. (We mention later, in the chapters which follow, the *qualitative* support that finance obtains, from the facilitation usually provided by the capitalist state and the related political process, both of which most often are in alliance with corporate capital and finance.) The high-value contribution of finance as a component of the services sector, however, goes with other relatively low-value activities which comprise the remaining share of services to GDP. Chapter 2 also analyses the status of countries under *subordina*-tion, with the liberalized market acting as an agency to extract and transfer surpluses to big capital located in advanced nations, and to international financial institutions where the power of advanced nations is rather supreme.

Emphasis laid as above on the role of deregulated finance in bringing about a state of subordination opposes the mainstream point of view which considers liberalization as a major tool for achieving efficiency. This comes from the 'efficient market' hypothesis – with rational agents supposed to operate with full knowledge, having 'rational expectations' in liberalized (and free) markets.

Paradoxically, the so-called free market, while incapable of achieving efficiency, has rather been instrumental in bringing about a divide among countries across the globe – by enabling the advanced countries to transact business to their advantage. The market played a major role here, by steering the course of liberal economic policies in the developing countries and gearing them in directions that were of benefit to the advanced countries. Unlike its assumed neutrality in mainstream economics, the market in reality brought unequal power relations between the rich advanced countries and the developing countries in the periphery. Finance played a major and dominant role across countries by enabling monopolistic pricing while supporting surplus extractions and their transfer from the developing countries. The market also exercised informal pressure on the developing countries to adopt neoliberal policies, much to the benefit of the advanced nations. In effect, the so-called free or deregulated financial market trailed the prevailing pattern of subordination faced by countries, which thus remained far removed from equal power relations between countries.

The chapter concludes by drawing attention to the heterodox and alternate formulations, many of which are relevant, in the following chapters on specific countries. The heterodox positions have been useful for interpreting the persisting stagnation and instability in the real economies of those countries, which is often accompanied by an ongoing boom in their financial sectors. The analysis provided in these chapters relies on the major Post-Keynesian critiques of the 'efficient market' principle and the later contribution of Keynes (in 1937) on the 'finance motive', which draws a distinction between the liquidity demand for purchase of equities subject to uncertainty and liquidity demand to purchase fixed return bonds.

The above is followed by an analysis in chapter 2 of uncertainty in Post-Keynesian economics, which remains the centrepiece of their writings.

Looking at Post-Keynesian writings and their relevance cannot be complete short of a consideration of the notion of 'fundamental uncertainty', which of late has been used to explain severe instability in economies. The chapter also refers back to Marx's notion of 'fictitious capital' which, despite methodological differences from related positions, still works as a major revelation for interpreting uncertainty and instability in capitalist economies.

Finally, questioning the validity of monetarist policies as tools to attain market efficiency, their analysis includes 'financialization' as a major offshoot of liberalized finance in the EMEs and other developing countries. Emphasis is similarly laid on institutional changes as facilitators of the financial sector – a point that goes well with our discussion of the political support for financialization in the last chapter of the book.

The conceptual tools as discussed in chapter 2 aim to provide the reader with a *background of the methodology* followed in our analysis of the major EMEs as offered in the chapters that follow.

Our analysis in chapters 3 and 4, which examine the experiences of major EMEs located in Latin America and Asia, highlight the routes to subordination that prevails over the developing countries in general. It is pointed out that many of these processes rely on the monetary-fiscal as well as exchange rate and reserve accumulation policies, and have consequences which are largely opposed to the domestic concerns of the developing countries.

Chapter 3 deals with Argentina, Brazil and Mexico, the three EMEs in Latin America we have chosen to analyse. Capital accounts in these countries were opened relatively early as compared to other developing countries. In dealing with the related changes that took place in these countries, we rely on our critique of the neoliberal policy prescriptions as given in chapter 2 of the book. We interpret the failures of the neoliberal policies in terms of the alternate methods suggested by heterodox

Post-Keynesian analysis. *Chapter 4* analyses the experiences of two relatively high-growth EMEs of Asia – China and India – which similarly have been recipients of large capital inflows from overseas and subject to higher growth rates. Unlike China, which of late has been showing some degree of course correction for maintaining autonomy in its policies, India, like the EMEs of South America, continues to be subject to a subordinated status.

We dwell on the specific patterns of financial subordination in these EMEs of Latin America and Asia in the process of their integration with global financial markets under the wave of globalization during the early 1990s. Our analysis reiterates the paradox between the low real growth rates and booming financial activities in these countries. Through this, we trace the *routes* of the subordination process, much of which relies on changes in the monetary-fiscal as well as exchange rate and reserve accumulation policies. These changes have been largely detrimental to the domestic interests of the developing countries. We try to provide specifics rather than broad directions, which we believe will help in providing complete answers to questions we raise on the futility of financial flows to bring growth in real terms. By looking at the specifics rather than limiting ourselves to the broad outline, we also hope to provide a complete picture of the countries' subordinated status that works against their real growth and welfare.

Finally, in *chapter 5*, the book reiterates the futility of free capital markets, with a dominance of finance, as tools for combating the contemporary crisis in capitalist economies. The chapter ends with an analysis of the socio-political processes behind in the developing areas in general, including in the EMEs. We make the point that while the quantitative weight of finance in terms of its turnover in the market lends it power over the rest of the economy, it is the political support of the state and the social process – which has gone through transformations with the decay of social capital – that works to further push finance to its commanding height in the economy.

This book considers the deregulation of markets as a major factor behind the elevation of finance to its present state of dominance in capitalist economies, resulting in detrimental effects on growth and welfare in real terms. We point out how, in the process of transformations as stated above, the developing areas of the world experienced a subordinated status, defined in terms of a lack of autonomy in the implementation of their domestic economic policies. The rather dismal picture that emerges brings back the relevance of imperialism, in a formal or informal (clandestine) capacity, over time.[2]

Notes

[1] Keynes (1937).

[2] For some articles with similar analysis, see Sen and Marcuzzo, eds (2018). See also, U. Patnaik and P. Patnaik (2016).

2

Mainstream Economic Theory for Financial Deregulation
Heterodox Economics as Alternative

Economic policies in developing counties often conform to policy prescriptions which follow the theoretical principles of mainstream economics. The underlying methodology is often viewed as sermons in developing countries, and are used to justify the steady opening up as well as the increased mobility of their capital markets. The implementation of policies including deregulation and related changes has been especially relevant in the emerging market economies (EMEs), which have been receiving large inflows of overseas capital since a long time.

We provide first, a few precepts of the early neoliberal methodology relating to the prediction of probability. This is relevant in the context of the use of normal distribution functions for probability calculation in financial markets in general.

FUTURE EVENTS CAN BE PREDICTED BY RELYING ON THE CALCULATION OF PROBABILITY: NEOLIBERAL POSITION

In most developing countries, justifications made to deregulate financial markets usually rely on the goal in mainstream economics of attaining 'market efficiency'. This in turn is based on assumptions of 'rational choice' on the part of all economic agents in the market who are assumed to have full knowledge of the changes in it. The arguments indicate capacity on the part of the agents to predict the future by making use of an ergodic probability function, which permits prediction of the future based on the frequency of past events.

Looking at the major tenets of mainstream economics and the policies which follow, we see that the early formulations there were based on the Benthamite cardinal (or statistical) notions of probability estimation, which relied on a frequency approach for calculating probability.

An Early Critique by Keynes (1921)

Keynes rejected the utilitarian notion in the cardinal estimates of utility in his book titled *The Treatise on Probability* (henceforth *Treatise*), published in 1921. He pointed out that probability relations are both logical and rational-objective. In this relation (between logical and rational-objective probability), Keynes spelt out the 'degree' of belief (α) in terms of the actual observations (a) relative to the diaspora of knowledge (h). For him, the probability relation $\alpha = a/h$ had to be based on the rational degree of belief under 'objective' conditions which was 'not subject to human "caprice"'.[1] This was in relation to the 'weight' of new evidence with additions to knowledge (h_1), which contributes to the probability relation (α) such that $\alpha = a/(h+h_1)$.

Most importantly, Keynes here draws attention to the fact that h and h_1 are not necessarily linked.[2] This is because the new pieces of evidence (h_1), while adding to the 'weight' when 'relevant', may not necessarily contribute to enhancing the degree of probability (α). As Keynes pointed out, situations may exist where such additional evidence remains irrelevant and the weight of the added evidence ($h+h_1$) remains unchanged. Thus, 'the weight ... measures the sum of the favourable and unfavourable evidence, [while] the probability measures the difference ... a new piece of evidence which leaves the balance unchanged, also leaves the probability of the argument unchanged.'[3]

Attention may be drawn here to an important aspect of this

formulation, which so far has remained unnoticed. Keynes' emphasis on the relevance of additional evidence for probability relations opens up an important counterpoint relating to the mainstream econometric models of probability estimations based on the cross-section or time-series data. From what is pointed out above, it turns out that extensions of a statistical series over a wider time-span or over a set of larger observations (which is 'additional knowledge') do not necessarily result in probability estimates that are more accurate. We also find that Keynes, citing Pierre Simon Laplace (a French mathematician of the previous century), states that 'probability is affected partly by our ignorance and partly by our knowledge'.[4] The point we make here may be treated as an additional critique of methods in econometrics that are frequently used to estimate the impact of neoliberal policies on economies. Finally, we also draw attention to the fact that the earlier and pre-Keynesian formulations of probability calculation rule out the impact of conventions and institutions on the behaviour patterns of agents and levels of uncertainty in markets.

Keynes, in his magnum opus, *The General Theory* (1936),[5] offered an alternate approach to probability relations under uncertainty. This was in terms of probability having a subjective base, and being driven by the 'animal spirits' of agents operating in the market. We observe that by reformulating, in 1921, the notion of calculable probability, Keynes had already anticipated the subjective elements as the core of his argument which came later in 'animal spirits'. He made it more explicit as follows: 'the alternate interpretation [of] "animal spirits ... [is] ... the spontaneous urge for action rather than inaction and not the outcome of a weighted average of quantitative benefits multiplied by quantitative averages"'.[6]

By putting 'animal spirits' as the prime mover for investments in markets and subject to changes that 'we do not know', Keynes as well as his followers in the Post-Keynesian tradition placed uncertainty at centre stage of the changes in deregulated markets.

THE EFFICIENT MARKET HYPOTHESIS
AS A TOOL FOR STOCK TRADING

The 'efficient market' hypothesis in mainstream economics has been used to guide stock-trading practices on the basis of the Black–Scholes–Merton (BSM) call-put formula, as well as in capital asset pricing models (CAPMs).

The rational choice assumption of mainstream economics has provided the basis for the call-put option-pricing formula, a tool popularly used by agents in stock markets. Used to predict the margins of gains/losses on bids for calls or puts in option trading, options are used as strategies to decide on investments in the stock market. The agents, while relying on tools as above, use 'rational choice' and an ergodic probability function to enable calculation of the probability of future stock-price movements. In this the future gets intractably linked to the past, since the weights attributed to past events continue to determine the probabilities of future outcomes, an assumption which completely rules out uncertainty.

Moreover, as pointed out by critics, the BSM formula to decide on stock options relies on calculations which use the standard deviations relating to the log-normal of stock prices. Thus, the formula assumes a normal distribution function for stock prices over time – which is highly unrealistic in markets subject to uncertainty.

Incidentally, in such formulations as above, option prices – and the corresponding premium on calls – are pitched higher with increases in stock-price volatility, which of course is subject to normal distribution function over time.[7] It may be pointed out that by relying on a formula as above, agents in the markets indicate an inclination to prefer increased volatility, causing more instability in markets – all in a bid to jack up option prices and to push the related premiums on calls with profits, and also to provide opportunities for shorting. Such inclinations may be considered as contributory factors to the turmoil in financial markets.

ALTERNATE APPROACHES TO INVESTMENT DECISIONS: KEYNES AND POST-KEYNESIANS

Tools as above in mainstream economics to arrive at investment decisions in economies have been questioned by Keynes and the Post-Keynesian economists (PKEs). Those formulations assume away uncertainty, which, according to Keynes and other heterodox economists, remains the *sine qua non* of changes in deregulated markets. For them, it is thus natural that deregulated financial flows will generate uncertainty in the market over time.

The Keynesian position incorporating uncertainty has been followed up by Post-Keynesians to explain recurrent crises, which also include the global financial crisis of 2007–09; while drawing attention to the contractionary effects that inflation-targeting policies of monetarism had in further dampening aggregate demand.

As already mentioned, the methodology of mainstream economics also gave the stock market a tool based on the BSM formula to predict returns on stocks.[8] Predictability of the future, as claimed in these formulations, enables agents to calculate returns on their investments in the market.[9] It does not come as a surprise that most of those decisions, based on an inappropriate notion of probability calculation, fail to provide a correct estimate of returns on investments. The consequences that follow include systemic instabilities and crises in the global economy.

The heterodox critique of the mainstream position on market efficiency rests, as the major issue, on the 'rational choice' assumption on the part of the agents while making investment decisions in markets. In effect, it relies on the calculation of probability by ruling out uncertainty – despite it being the *sine qua non* of all decision-making processes, which amounts to a denial of realities in the market.[10]

Assumptions relating to rational expectations and subjective calculation of probability are also used in mainstream theory to estimate security prices by using the CAPMs in the market. Critiques of this approach, along with those of the BSM formula in estimating call-put margins, relate to their underlying position of a static equilibrium with no endogenous movement. The assumptions of these positivist models, which continued to be defended by the Chicago economist Milton Friedman, were questioned by Post-Keynesian economists on grounds of their lack of realism.[11]

Deregulation of finance, as pointed out by the critiques, has been largely responsible for the expansion of financial activities subject to short-termism and instabilities. The related flows of capital contributed to what is described as financialization, with financial assets providing returns higher than those of non-financial (real) assets. The surges in financial activities in the global economy can be attributed to uncritical adherence on the part of the official agencies to mainstream prescriptions for financial deregulation.

However, under deregulation of financial markets, the state often pitches the domestic interest rate high and keeps the exchange rate of domestic currency overvalued by appreciating it. Both, in effect, push up the prices of financial assets in terms of domestic currency. While the higher interest rates and the appreciated exchange rates continue to attract further inflows of overseas capital, the higher rates of interest bring in higher returns on financial assets held in domestic currency. Such measures help finance, which is in alliance with the state under contemporary capitalism, but those are detrimental to the interests of the real economy of the concerned countries. The implicit directives of monetarist policies as above turn out to be measures which benefit overseas finance.

We need to remember that the limit placed on credit expansion by using high rates of interest remains an important tool to curb inflation under monetarism. Use there is made of inflation-targeting with a credit and fiscal squeeze while the exchange rate of domestic currency in the market tends to appreciate as a result of capital inflows entering the market. Attempts by the monetary authorities to avoid exchange rate appreciation by purchasing foreign currency leads to a rise in exchange reserves (high-powered money), causing an expansion in domestic credit. This has led to the frequent use of inflation-targeting by monetary authorities. However, appreciation of the exchange rate is also considered conducive to larger inflows of overseas finance, by generating expectations of a further rise in financial asset prices denominated in the appreciating currency. This obviously goes contrary to the interests of the real economy, especially industry, which loses its competitiveness vis-à-vis foreign goods.

As for possible depreciation of exchange rates which has been more common in the developing countries, it causes inflation which is often sought to be rectified by following inflation-targeting policies that bring with it, recession and unemployment.

The lack of autonomy implicit in the choice of policies on interest rates and exchange rates indicates a *state of subordination* in capital-importing economies, arising from their inability to choose policies which can be of help to their domestic economies.

Incidentally, it is relevant that getting interest rates 'right', which is one of the major goals in line with neoliberal precepts, has been pursued by international financial institutions like the World Bank over the last few decades.[12] All in all, the alliance between finance and the state in advanced countries is being strengthened further through the support of international financial institutions which by and large are controlled by the advanced countries.

The lack of autonomy on the part of developing countries is also apparent in their failed attempts to regulate interest rates when exchange rates are managed under liberalized capital flows. The syndrome, described as 'impossible trinity',[13] relates to the typical *trilemma* faced by countries when capital flows are liberalized and the exchange rate is subject to official control (or management). This is because free capital flows may induce a rise or drop in the exchange rate of the domestic currency; while to limit those changes in the exchange rate the monetary authorities need to adjust the interest rate by pushing it up or down. The outcome is one where the monetary authorities lose autonomy over domestic monetary policy, which is *one more instance of subordination* to the diktats of neoliberal norms advocated by overseas official as well as private financial agencies.

Post-Keynesian Critiques and Related Analysis

Questioning deregulation in financial markets on grounds of their goal of attaining efficiency, critiques in the Keynesian tradition highlight the neglect of *uncertainty* in mainstream formulations. This argument has been a cornerstone of further analysis in Post-Keynesian economics.[14]

Liberalization of overseas capital flows contributed to large flows of short-term capital, combined with high risks, fetching high returns in markets. This led to tendencies in markets to invest more on financials than on assets backed by real activities – resulting in 'financialization' with the backing of an overpowering financial sector. The pattern has prevailed in the majority of the EMEs analysed in the following chapters.

It seems pertinent to raise a question here that relates to the unknown pattern (or composition) of investment that could emerge in the above context. One may ask whether additional investments in financial assets can continue over time under rising degrees of uncertainty. The answer hinges on the impact of the growing uncertainty on the composition of investments, especially relating to the acquisition of financial assets with higher rates of return in the market. The answer rests on a reference to 'fundamental uncertainty', which we analyse below.

Fundamental Uncertainty – A Deadlock Inside
the Tunnel – Global Financial Crisis

We now address what Post-Keynesians synthesized as 'fundamental uncertainty', a position that has been subject to debate.[15] As has been pointed out while seeking an identification of fundamental uncertainty, problems which arise in predicting the future are neither related to the cognitive limitations of the agents, nor to their lack of capacity to handle or access technology as under 'bounded rationality'.[16] Rather, it is because of the fact that the future itself keeps changing and gets shaped by the actors' own actions.[17] In effect, the 'agent does not choose from a given list of possibilities, but actually creates the list'.[18] To be more specific, decisions taken in the light of expectations or conventions in today's short-period equilibrium continually bring in a new short-period situation. As pointed out by Joan Robinson, 'to develop an analysis which throws light it is necessary to get rid of the concept of equilibrium and substitute historical time, in which the ever-moving present separates an irrevocable past from an uncertain future'.[19]

Arguments such as above pertain to what has been described in the literature as 'fundamental uncertainty' – a notion which relates to 'the unknowability of the future, to creative human agency and the unique nature of unfolding time'.[20] The notion amounts to a 'lack of determinacy as an ontological property of the universe, with imprecise knowledge as an epistemic property of agents in that universe'.[21] As succinctly put by Davidson, Keynes' concept of uncertainty reflects the future as 'transmutable or creative in the sense that future economic outcomes may be permanently changed … by the actions today of individuals, groups and/or governments, often in ways that are not even perceived by the creators of change'.[22]

This is in tune with what Keynes had famously interpreted as '… uncertain knowledge [by which] I do not mean merely to distinguish what is known for certain from what is probable. ... About these matters there is no scientific basis on which to form any calculable probability whatever. We simply do not know.'[23] Further, fundamental uncertainty of the Keynesian variety, as pointed out by Shiela Dow, 'allows analysis of differing degrees of uncertainty and the cognitive role of institutions and conventions'.[24]

Keynes used the term 'ignorance' to refer to lack of evidence relative to availability of evidence, which 'is a matter of degree. ... This is because although risk is calculable with certainty, uncertainty is generated by ignorance, which, again according to Shiela Dow, amounts to a "lack of evidence relative to availability of evidence".'[25] To repeat, thus, uncertainty is a matter of degree.

From the above it does not require much to conclude that in *General Theory*, Keynes was very much in line with the notion of fundamental uncertainty, which, under non-ergodic conditions, rules out precise predictions of the future. This goes with the fact that, as mentioned in the context of fundamental uncertainty, with 'creativity' of actions by investors, new realities come up as 'potential surprises'.[26]

It is relevant here to point out that the investment decisions of individual agents, continually influenced by business sentiments prevailing in the market, are also considerably shaped by actions on the part of those who operate in a similar manner.[27] The pattern is akin to Keynes' metaphor of a 'beauty contest', where opinions are formed on the basis of what others (judges) consider to be beautiful. The average view that emerges can be described as 'convention', with the investor influenced by the subjective confidence (or weight) attributed to such conventions.

Incidentally, while the respective demand for long-term financial as well as real assets are generally more when their respective returns move up, for short-term financial assets the demand as well as returns remain susceptible to the volatilities caused by uncertainty. Thus, the returns on short-term financial assets can move only with uncertainty in markets, providing opportunities of both gains and losses to the agents.[28]

However, changes in the returns on financial assets, while positive up to some level of uncertainty, can turn negative when the uncertainty crosses a limit that relates to a situation of fundamental uncertainty. One finds here a parallel to the Minskian state of Ponzi finance with borrowers unable to reschedule debt liabilities by borrowing fresh in an uncertain market, which is due to fundamental uncertainty.

Thus, the expanding financial sector, along with the shrinkage in the share and growth of the real sector, may typically generate a path which at some stage is likely to encounter a roadblock under excessive degrees of uncertainty. It is not difficult to trace such situations, given the experience of the global financial crisis of 2008–09 and the great recession that followed it.

We make use, in chapters 3 and 4, of conceptual issues as stated above. We attempt, in these chapters, to rely on relevant Post-Keynesian and Marxist formulations to explain the ongoing instability and stagnation in real economies as experienced by the major EMEs of Latin America and Asia.

'FICTITIOUS CAPITAL' IN MARX

This brings us back to returns on financial assets which include dividends and capital gains in the stock market as well as interest earned on loans or public debt/bonds – all of which depend on their possible materialization in the future, which remains uncertain. These returns are subject to a special trait, namely the alienation of financial transactions from the production process. This makes financial flows circulate in search of profits along a *circuitous route* which bypasses production, charting out a path that relates to what Marx observed as *M–M' rather than M–C–M'*.[29]

The above characterization by Marx, which relates to the

prevailing institutions in his time, bears a generality which captures the currents of contemporary capitalism, especially in the context of the *alienation* of finance from the production *process*. Marx's characterization is identified in heterodox literature as one that reflects the properties of 'fictitious finance'.[30]

Dwelling further on the sources of alienated finance in economies, we draw attention to categories of returns which can be described as 'rentier income'. The latter includes dividends, capital gains in stock markets, and also interest rates on loans, public debt as well as bonds. Such returns remain distant from activities which generate real income and employment, pre-empting additions to consumption, wage income or productive investment. These are also the flows of fictitious capital as mentioned above, which moves along a circuit where wealth is created only for those having the ability as well as prior access to purchases of financial assets, and can also use those as collaterals for leveraging. None of these activities come close to the sphere of real activities.

Structural Change and Its Economic Dynamics: The Rise of Finance to Dominance

Changes in the structural pattern have been prominent within most economies since their integration with global finance started in the early 1990s. These changes, initiated by deregulated capital flows, include variations in the sector-wise composition of aggregate output that have taken place in economies, particularly since the 2008–09 global financial crisis.

The changes include the faster pace of growth in the services sector and in its contribution to the gross domestic product (GDP). This can be compared to the growth rates in industry which failed to recover in most countries at the end of the global recession. As already mentioned, the services sector includes a large share of the *value* of financial services, which is largely due to *high-value* financial transactions. The large share of the services sector in GDP is thus matched by a similarly large contribution of financial services to GDP. This makes for the *quantitative significance of finance* in economies, in particular in the post-global financial crisis years. We refer to the *qualitative aspects* of the facilitating factors (for finance), mostly offered by the state, later in this chapter.

Historically, the process by which the financial sector assumed the lead role in terms of its quantitative weight, which led to its power in the economy, was initiated in the United States with the passing of the Gramm–Leach–Bliley (GLB) Act in 1999 ending the prevailing restrictions on banks in handling securities. Till then, under the Glass–Stegall Act of 1933, banks in the USA were restrained from dealing with securities. The GLB Act marked a major turning point with the ascendancy of finance which gradually spread to the rest of world including the developing regions and emerging market economies as discussed in this book.

The dynamics of structural changes in economies get reflected in the changing sector-wise contribution of their output. Of those, the rise in the share of the financial sector to the GDP can be attributed to the high prices of financial assets relative to other components in the services sector.

Financial activities along with the financial sector as a whole operate as prime movers in markets within economies. The reasons include, apart from the relatively high rates of returns on financial assets, changes in the socio-political environment of countries which have been accommodative.[31] Thus, there prevails a *circuitous link* between the socio-political and economic forces in the country on the one hand, and the structural dynamics of its economy on the other. Accordingly, changes in the quantitative and qualitative significance (or weights) of finance, which reflect power relations across different sectors of the economy, push up the status of finance in economies.

Going by the analysis of structural dynamics in economies,

it has been pointed out that it is the relative profitability that guides investment decisions of capitalists, and that such motives also work as the prime mover of the changes that take place.[32] Further, the process of such changes or the path of the 'traverse' relies, for given resources and the technological status of an economy, on the pattern of interdependence between the different sectors within it, which can be subject to vertical or horizontal configurations.[33]

Interactions as above between different sectors of an economy at successive stages provide, in principle, the necessary condition to ensure continuity of the process along sectors. The outcome of the latter, in reality, may take a different turn with conflicting interests between individual sectors which are opposed to each other. In such cases, it is the relative weight of individual sectors as shaped and nurtured by socio-political and economic forces in the country that works as the deciding factor to determine the final outcome.[34]

The analysis suggests that structural changes in economies can be interpreted by underlying alliances or their absence between different sectors. The outcome, as under the Braudelian multidimensional horizon, continues to shape the specific direction of the changes according to the possible constellation of the respective weights relating to different sectors.[35]

The *rise of finance to dominance* over other sectors, often witnessed in economies, can also pass through situations of conflict between social groups and financial interests, especially in developing countries. These conflicts could arise, for instance, on issues like the displacement of people at construction sites of mega infrastructure projects, often funded by financial conglomerates. In such situations the state often takes the side of big financial capital, which inevitably brings benefits to its ally, the financial sector.

Institutional Changes, Deregulated Finance and the Notion of 'New Capital'

Interpreting further the structural changes that come about with deregulated finance, we move to describe a stage of capitalism that we identify as '*new capital*'.[36] The state here actively sponsors the reforms in the ongoing legal system and in institutions to help the financial sector. Spread across the globe, 'new capital' also relies on alliances between the powerful elite and the state in each country, often both in close proximity to global finance and the multinational financial agencies.

It is not difficult to locate the impact of these alliances on related institutional changes in economies, especially in the emerging market economies (EMEs). With the systemic crises appearing at frequent intervals, one can witness a passive acceptance or at best a noticeable inaction on the part of the regulatory authorities when it comes to the need for mitigating the frequency of similar happenings. Such inaction made way for greater concentration within the banking industry along with the rampant use of hedging instruments in risky ventures.

The state in these countries has often been described as 'predatory',[37] promoting a benign neglect of the consequences resulting from collusive agreements between big corporations. All this acts in the interests of finance, enhancing the *quantitative* expanse as well as the weight and power of the financial sector in the economy.

Changes as mentioned above and similar others indicate the apathy in the socio-political regime of what we identify as 'new capital', towards issues related to a dismal growth in output, employment and spread of social welfare in the economy. There is an embedded and institutionalized political and economic process, where the industrial as well as agricultural sectors have little access to the privileges doled out by the state to finance. This is also reflected in the steady increase in the informalization of jobs in the developing countries, often at wages below subsistence level and with poverty-stricken people in the lowest strata of the Braudelian 'triptych'.[38] Here labourers continue to strive to obtain the basic needs of material well-being while failing to achieve remuneration at comparable rates in the market. Situations such as these which emerge, especially in the developing countries, do not matter as concerns either for the nation state or for its ally, 'new capital'.

As already mentioned, the institutional changes which followed deregulated finance, within and across countries, included the following. *First*, changes in the segregated status of banks to universal banking which permitted them access to security trading. Unlike what prevailed under deposit-led segregated banking practices, banks under universal banking were enabled to trade as well as invest in financial assets like securities and derivatives which could be exchanged in the secondary stock markets. Banks also could underwrite the trading of securities in over-the-counter (OTC) trading outside formal exchanges, providing an additional, major channel for transactions of securities. In effect, banks started earning more from trading activities in the market than from advances of credit led by deposits.

The ongoing deregulation of financial markets, concurrent with uncertainty as expected, made it difficult to predict future earnings on investments. This brought the *second* institutional change with the use of derivatives as hedging instruments to guard against risks in the trading of financial assets under uncertainty. Those transactions were over and above the old stocks transacted in the secondary market of stock exchange.

Third, with uncertainty growing further on the possibilities of gains or losses, there came up further demands for derivatives – ranging from forwards, futures, options, swaps and the like – generating liquidity demand to meet what Keynes observed in 1937 as the 'finance motive'. Derivatives, as with equity shares, also were traded on the basis of expected gains or losses, which often remained unfulfilled. The requisite supply of liquidity to meet demand was provided by inflows of short-term capital, as under endogenous money.

Adding to the demands for liquidity as already mentioned above, the asset-based securitizations (ABSs) made for new channels to leverage, providing further access to liquidity. In all, deregulated finance has worked both for additional *demand* for liquidity as well as the ballooning of liquidity *supplied* to the financial market which continues to circulate at risk. In the meantime, expansions of the real economy continue to be negligible or are non-existent.

The *fourth* major institutional change in the financial market under deregulation is marked by the entry of non-financial corporates (NFCs) in the security market. Their marked presence is reflected in the large share of financial assets in portfolios held by NFCs.[39] The participation of banks as well as NFCs in the financial market makes way for larger flows of transactions in such markets, as can be seen from the rising capitalization of stock markets.

As already mentioned earlier in this chapter, the circulation of finance based on transactions of equity shares and other financial assets normally encounters risks which are related to uncertainty. An example as to how the related risk is handled can be provided by looking at the way the equity share prices get determined in the market.

The price at which an equity share is sold depends on the discounted value of its expected returns – the latter calculated as the sum of dividends accrued over time and the profit expected from the capital gains realized on its sales price. But in deregulated financial markets, both the dividend rate and profit rate remain uncertain, and their probability or likelihood is subject to guesstimates on the part of those who transact. In the meantime, changes in the discount rate due to variations in interest rates in the market also affect such calculations.

Subordinate Economic Status of Neo-Colonies: Further Interpretations in Heterodox Economics

We have attempted to provide, in the present chapter, an analytical account of the subordinate status of neo-colonies in the context of contemporary capitalism. Most of those neo-colonies were subject to subordination during their colonial past by foreign rulers using controls rather than through the liberalization of financial flows as the major tool for expropriating financial surpluses from their colonies.[40] The pattern of economic subordination currently experienced by neo-colonies of the global South, which prevails despite their political independence, relies on a liberalized market for cross-border capital flows. The analysis in this chapter, and later in chapters 3 and 4 with country details, brings to the fore the major role played by liberalized flows of capital in making the transfers abroad operational.

For countries receiving liberalized inflows of capital, in the event of the flows getting interrupted by newly introduced restrictions, there emerges the threat of possible reversals leading to outflows of capital. The possible menace of fund withdrawals has been effective enough to keep a check on the capital-importing countries from initiating any restraining measure relating to flows of overseas capital. Of those flows, short-term portfolio capital rather than long-term FDI is more susceptible to quick reversals as above. But FDI is also affected, over time, by such policy moves. While short-term inflows remain the regular sources for financing the hedging instruments provided by derivatives (which have no contribution to output and real activities), those flows also contribute foreign exchange to the economy. Its impact on the exchange rate of domestic currency, as mentioned earlier, is often mitigated by the state with purchase of foreign currency in the market and entering it as official reserves. A sudden reversal of capital inflows, both for short-term and long-term FDIs, resulting from newly imposed restraints on free flows may thus put the capital-importing economy in trouble, especially with the concerns often voiced by the global credit rating agencies relating to the solvency of the capital-importing countries.

The impact of situations such as above on the globally integrated capital-importing countries makes them face the issue of a loss of autonomy while framing domestic policies. This arises from the fact that those restraints may include a departure from the mainstream policy of inflation-targeting or even the managing of domestic exchange rates to reach levels which benefit the real economy rather than the financial activities. The inability of policymakers to follow such a course, with the reality of the threat perception, is perceived in this book as *subordination*. Despite the limitations of neoliberal formulations, such theories have occupied a major space in policymaking by a large number of developing economies including EMEs. This relates to the use of monetarist prescriptions for price stability by using inflation-targeting.

We have pointed out, in the chapters which follow with country details, how the application of monetarist policies has been responsible for consequences such as stagnation with austerity and volatility in the respective economies. The outcome generally has been to the benefit of investors having prior access to financial assets, mostly drawn from overseas. The policies adopted are facilitated by alliances between the state in developing countries and financial agencies in advanced economies, helping to expedite the process of expropriation from the subordinated nations.

Changes in financial market transactions in countries under deregulated finance usually get reflected in: (i) rapid increases in credit as ratio to GDP; (ii) a rise in profits on financial transactions as shares of aggregate profits – both for banks and non-banking financial companies (NBFCs); (iii) rising capitalization of stock exchanges reflecting a rise in the trading of shares; and (iv) multiple layers of hedging instruments which consist of exchange-traded as well as OTC instruments. One needs to recognize here the role of market volatility in generating the risks to be covered by hedging instruments, with additional liquidity demand for derivatives transactions which relates to Keynes' 'finance motive'. In this short-term capital flows have been the main source for funding derivative instruments, which contributed to additional volatility.

While uncertainty, by initiating volatility, makes for further changes in the market, there may be a dead-end when the market expansions can no longer continue. Such a situation brings back a scenario of downward slides in the market, for instance, as happened during the global financial crisis with a collapse of financial as well as real transactions, initially in the US and later followed by brisk contagion effects spreading all over the globe.

For the Post-Keynesians, crisis situations as above are subject to fundamental uncertainty when the degree of unknowability (or uncertainty) cumulates over time, which was often due to the actions of agents in markets. The major cause has been, as pointed out, the uncritical acceptance of neoliberal economic policies which ignores uncertainty while promoting the dominant role and status of finance in economies.

As already mentioned, dominance of the financial sector can be related to structural changes in the economy, which include the rising share of the services sector in GDP and the simultaneous rise of finance as a component of services. This goes with the *quantitative* expansion of financial activities in the economy, achieving concurrent power over the whole economy. The power of finance also gets augmented by *qualitative* support with facilitation offered by the state and the social set-up. In this, the state comes up as an ever-ready promoter, which makes it rather easy for finance to ride to its position of supremacy. Forces behind the *quantitative* expansion also include the relative attraction of investing in short-term financial assets fetching relatively high as well as quick returns which leads to financialization. Changes as above have transformed capitalism to its prevailing regime of 'new capital' in support of the dominant financial sector.

Explanations by the Marxist school also emphasize the *realization crisis*, pointing at the role of financial flows to provide outlets for profitable investments which are neither available in the real sector nor contribute to its expansion. In Marxist literature, earnings having their origin in the financial sector are identified as *fictitious capital*, with no capacity to generate activities or output in the real sectors of the economy. These earnings consist of rentier capital which is also identified in the Post-Keynesian literature as a category that is de-coupled from the real sector.

CONCLUSION

To sum up, we now focus on the *main theme* of the book, concerning the *subordinate status* of developing countries in the global South. In contrast to their colonial past when controls over financial flows remained the major tool of the ruling empires for expropriating financial surpluses from the colonies, subordination as experienced by developing countries under contemporary capitalism relies on deregulated financial flows. Supplemented by neoliberal policies which achieved neither stable nor efficient markets, the outcome most often brought austerity to benefit powerful overseas investors. Such policies rely on the ongoing alliances between national governments in the developing countries and financial agencies as well as the state in advanced economies, working to facilitate the process of their expropriation.

It is not difficult to pinpoint the specific policies in the monetarist framework which remain grossly inappropriate for the economies of the developing region. One can mention the enforcing of stiff interest rates and fiscal restraint, both responsible for further contractions in the developing countries which have been typically recession-prone. Managed exchange rates of domestic currency in those countries, following neoliberal precepts, are often set at too-high levels to attract flows of foreign capital, especially on short-term tenures. The package often reflected a combination of high interest rates and appreciated exchange rates, both contractionary in terms of aggregate demand in the recession-prone developing economies. On the whole, 'inflation-targeting' with fiscal and monetary restraints, instituted with blind faith in monetarism on the part of developing country governments, has brought detrimental consequences for their economies. Subordination also enforces similar other consequences, with free play of short-term portfolio capital in speculation by using derivatives. A similar one was the compulsive pressure on the state to add to official reserves on a precautionary basis. Examples of such subordinated status are provided in the next two chapters giving a detailed analytical account of some EMEs in Latin America and Asia.

The questioning of neoliberal methodology and policy as set out here has been used in the next two chapters to explain the dismal consequences faced by EMEs when under compulsion from overseas to implement strategies as above. The outcome, as we point out, has been the systemic crises faced by those economies with finance continuing its role as the dominant sector.

Critiques of the efficient market hypotheses, initially by Keynes in 1921 and later in 1936, and in Post-Keynesian Economics (PKE) of the heterodox schools in recent times, point out that there exists a need for subscribing to alternative approaches. The need is felt even more when we realize the actual impact of policies which were based on mainstream theory. Incapable of ensuring an efficient market as promised, subscribing to those policies can be held responsible for much of the instability and sluggish growth experienced by the subordinated developing economies.

The alternate approaches in the heterodox tradition, which includes PKE, rest on uncertainty as the main pillar to analyse and explain changes which were assumed away in mainstream analysis. Rising uncertainty has a major impact on the prices of financial assets by making them volatile, creating opportunities for profits.

Finally, deregulation of capital flows in particular can be held responsible for initiating uncertainty in financial markets, which generates risks as well as the use of hedging instruments. Returns on financial assets, especially on short-term categories, move up much higher than those on real-sector assets – making for what in the literature is described as *financialization*, with the rise of financial transactions relative to those related to other activities.

Identification of the specific points of inflection as provided in the next two chapters indicates how policymakers in the respective EMEs were often obliged to implement, often uncritically, the dictates of dominant finance – a pattern which reflects the path to subordination.

Analysis as above will hopefully fill the gaps which remain in literature on the subordinated status of the peripheral nations.

Notes

[1] Bateman and Davis (1991), p. 58.

[2] O'Donnell (1990).

[3] Keynes (1921), pp. 77–78, 84.

[4] *The Papers of John Maynard Keynes*, Archive Centre, King's College, Cambridge, TP/D/6.

[5] Keynes (1936).

[6] Ibid., pp. 161–62.

[7] We may refer here to the formula for call (buy) options. A more complete account of the mainstream formulation and its critique is available in Sen (2020).

[8] As pointed out, 'In terms of the assumptions underlying the formula for call-put (or buy-sell) options in terms of the BSM model, agents operating in markets rely on an ergodic probability function, which in turn makes the future intractably linked to the past, whereas weights attributed to past events continue to determine the probabilities of future outcomes' (Sen 2020, p. 270).

[9] Ibid.

[10] Davidson (2003), pp. 230–31; Saith (2022), pp. 329–67.

[11] Crotty (2013).

[12] Karwowski (2020).

[13] Fleming (1962).

[14] Mader, Mertens and Zwan (2020).

[15] Dunn (2001).

[16] Simon (1987).

[17] Dunn (2001), p. 578; Sen (2020), pp. 274–75.

[18] de Carvalho (1988).

[19] Robinson (1974), Robinson (1979). See also H.W. Singer in Sen (1996), pp. 102–10.

[20] Dunn (2008), p. 96.

[21] Brandolini, Dall'Aste and Scazzieri, eds (2011), p. 73.

[22] Davidson (2003), p. 234.

[23] Keynes (1936), pp. 235–36.

[24] Dow (2016), pp. 14–15

[25] Ibid.

[26] Rosser (2001), p. 547.

[27] David (1955).

[28] While we do not agree with the mainstream models which define stock market transactions in terms of call-put margins, one notices the role of higher standard deviation in stock prices as a factor which induces the rise in margins of calls and, in effect, volatility in uncertain markets.

[29] Marx (2016).

[30] Durand (2007). See also Harris (1988).

[31] Scazzieri (2022).

[32] Pasinetti (1963).

[33] Cardinale (2020).

[34] Sen (2023b).

[35] Braudel (1977), chapter II.

[36] The notion of 'new capital' came up in a discussion I had with Roberto Scazzieri in 2019 at Cambridge. I am grateful to him for the insightful discussions. The point is further clarified in his paper, Scazzieri (2022).

[37] Galbraith (2010).

[38] Braudel (1977), chapter II.

[39] Sen and Dasgupta (2014).

[40] Sen (1992); Sen (2023a).

3

Subordinating Financialization in Emerging Market Economies (EMEs) of Latin America

THE BACKGROUND

The spread of financialization, while similar between the advanced and developing economies in terms of the relative attraction for investments in finance, also has to consider the historical experiences of a large number of developing countries – initially as subjugated colonies and later transformed into neo-colonies under contemporary capitalism.

Finance during colonial rule worked as a useful tool for the ruling country to appropriate resources from the politically subjugated nations. The pattern of the *loot* (or misappropriation) which took place in India under British rule relied on *stringent controls* over the politically subordinated colony, which in effect strengthened the empire.[1] Contrasting this pattern under colonialism, the prevailing mode of surplus extraction under contemporary capitalism, largely consisting of rentier income as well as profit and other earnings procured from the capital-importing countries, relies on the *liberalization of finance*.

The present chapter dwells on three major emerging market economies (EMEs) of Latin America and enquires into the implications of liberalized capital flows under contemporary capitalism while pointing out how deregulated financial markets provided the agency to procure rentier incomes and profits for big financial corporates abroad. Such transfers of incomes can be identified as the Marxian notion of fictitious capital mentioned earlier.

With large volumes of cross-border capital flowing in the direction of the major economies of Latin America and Asia, their exposure to those flows happened to be higher as compared to that of other developing economies. This led to their nomenclature in the literature as EMEs without, however, displaying much 'emergence' in real terms of development in their economies.

Despite the limitations of the nomenclature, we choose to analyse the three major economies of Latin America – Brazil, Mexico and Argentina – as EMEs in this chapter. All three countries have had similar experiences as recipients of large volatile foreign funds that had an impact on their respective economies. We also consider, in the next chapter, China and India, the two large and high-growth EMEs of Asia.

The three EMEs of Latin America as above received large volumes of capital since an earlier time period as compared to the other countries in the region. The major factor behind this was the liberal financial policies which were initiated much earlier in these economies. As for the two EMEs of Asia, the growth rates of gross domestic product (GDP) have been relatively high in both China and India – and this, along with steady liberalization, helped to draw large flows of overseas capital into these countries. The three EMEs of Latin America, on the other hand, failed to attain high growth rates of GDP, for reasons that we try to explore below.

Deregulated finance had a major role in surplus extraction, which worked at the informal behest of overseas finance. Most often this also had the compliance of overseas governments. The implicit norms laid down in the liberalized markets included a revoke or reprisal on the part of the overseas financial institutions by initiating a reversal of flows. This could come about, as mentioned earlier, even with the slightest deviations in the official policies of host governments relating to free flow of overseas capital. Impending threats of crisis often persuaded domestic governments to continue with the liberalized flows.

The three large EMEs of Latin America we are dealing with can be observed to have drifted from one crisis to another, largely due to the volatility of unregulated flows of short-term capital which formed the major component of their aggregate capital flows. The reasons include the relative profitability in the investment of the short-term flows, with high returns to cover risk under uncertainty and their rapid turnover.

Under the subheadings for the three countries given below, we *first* offer an overview of the impact of the neoliberal fiscal-monetary package of inflation-targeting in the respective countries, with the austerity measures followed in all three of those. Attention is drawn to the systematic pattern of real stagnation and financial boom which was experienced.

We also highlight the structural dynamics that came into play in the three economies, including its impact in terms of elevating finance to a state of dominance over the rest of the economy. The underlying conceptual sequence has already been analysed in the previous chapter.

Next we document, under country perspectives, more detailed aspects of the *ongoing pattern of subordination* experienced by the individual countries. Much of this, as we point out, reflects the uneven power relations – between finance at its peak and dominance, and the rest of the stagnating host economy. Subordination also relates to the supreme authority of the free market in giving directions to their official policies to adhere to mainstream economics.

BOOMING FINANCE AND REAL STAGNATION

Economies subject to stagnation in GDP growth often have a booming financial sector. The pattern can be observed in both the advanced and the developing nations.

As for stagnation the GDP growth in the three EMEs of Latin

America has been rather moderate over the last four decades or more, subject to lower ranges as well as wider fluctuations, as can be seen in Figure 3.1.

As for the volatility in GDP growth, it can be observed that in Argentina, the growth of GDP fluctuated between (−)10.89 per cent and (+)10.12 per cent between 2002 and 2010. The situation in terms of both growth rate and volatility was no better in Brazil and Mexico, with the volatile GDP growth rates, even when positive, hardly exceeding 5 per cent since as early as the 1980s. The growth rates consistently turned negative in all three countries especially over the post-global financial crisis (GFC) years.

We now look at the flows of overseas capital for these countries and a few other indicators, like rising stock market capitalization and the financing of derivatives with short-run capital flows. These provide a further background for the divergent trajectory of their real economy and financial activities.

Net portfolio liabilities, as recorded in data sources, represent net inflows of short-term capital from overseas. These have been subject to noticeable fluctuations, subject to an upward trend for

FIGURE 3.1 *GDP growth rates in Argentina, Brazil, Mexico, percentage change, 1980–2000*

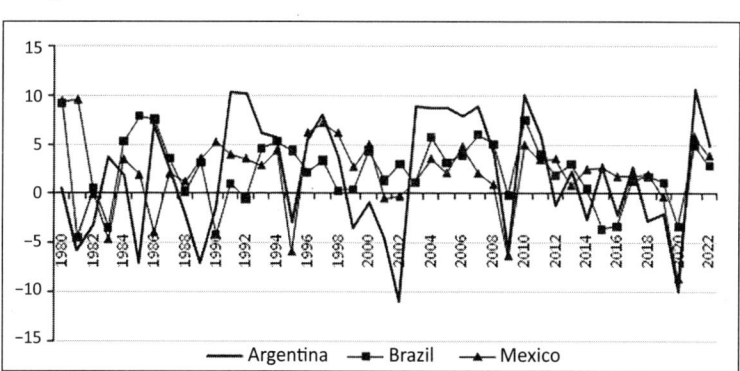

Source: International Monetary Fund (IMF), *World Economic Outlook Database*, October 2024.

FIGURE 3.2 *Net portfolio capital flows to Argentina, Brazil and Mexico, 1980–2022*

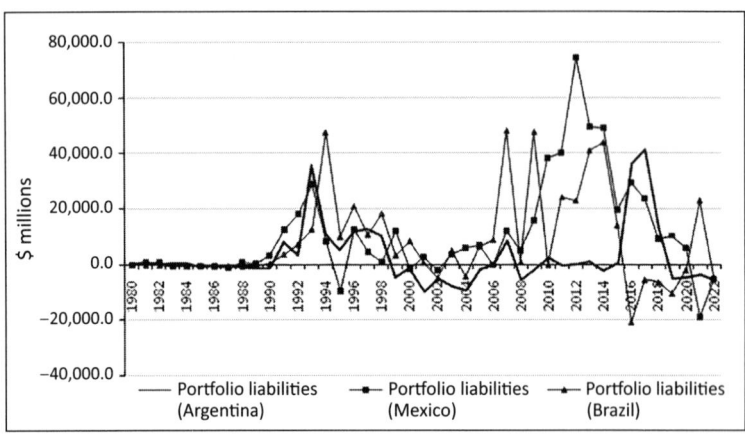

Source: As in Figure 3.1.

FIGURE 3.3 *Net flows of derivatives to Argentina, Brazil and Mexico, 1980–2022*

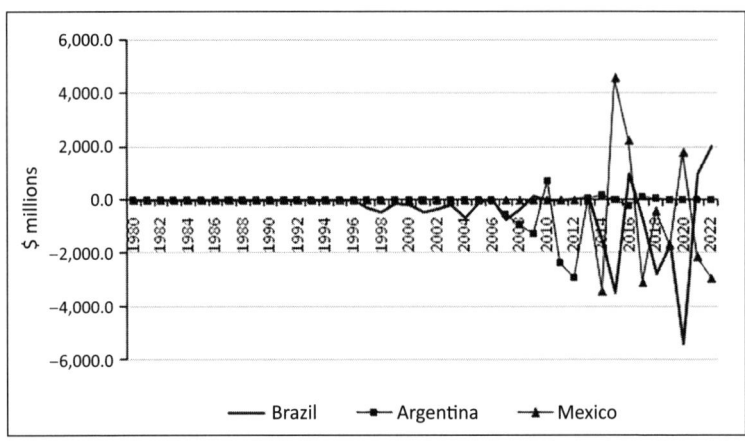

Source: As in Figure 3.1.

FIGURE 3.4 *Net FDI flows to Brazil, Argentina and Mexico, 1980–2022*

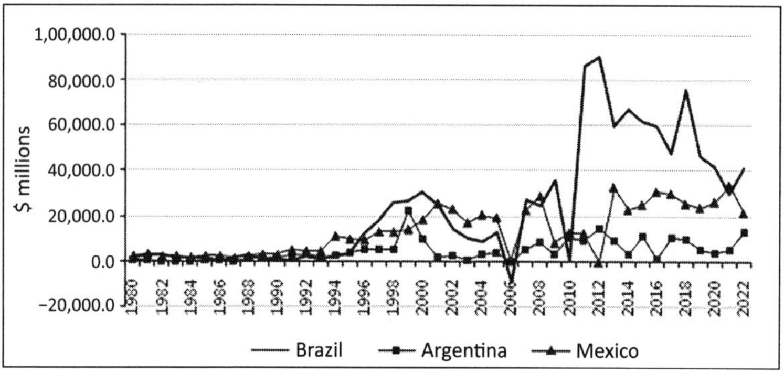

Source: As in Figure 3.1.

all three countries over the same decades. Interestingly, the sharp declines in net inflows that took place during the GFC were more than reversed in a few years with upturns in all three EMEs. The recovery seemed to be sharper for the short-term capital inflows as compared to FDI inflows.

Brazil, subject to wide magnitudes of volatility in short-term capital flows, experienced significant net outflows of portfolio capital between 2016 and 2020, with the last year marking the Covid-19 pandemic. Negative net flows of the same also prevailed for Argentina between 2020 and 2022. For Argentina and Mexico, net inflows (liabilities) of portfolio finance even exceeded the net foreign direct investment (FDI) inflows sometimes, indicating the embedded volatility of short-term capital. Brazil, however, had a different pattern with net FDI inflows far exceeding net portfolio flows. We explain the differences later under the country subheadings which follow.

That liberalization of capital flows somewhat facilitated direct investment as well can be observed in the moderately rising net FDI inflows to all three EMEs. As for net flows of FDI, the sums reaching Argentina and Mexico were similar while Brazil appears to be an outlier in terms of the amounts reaching it after 2011.

As pointed out by the critiques of neoliberal policies, the experiences of the three EMEs under deregulated finance can be linked to their blind adherence to neoliberal reforms which continued to be advocated from multiple sources. These sources included the multinational corporate sector in advanced economies, the Bretton Woods financial institutions, as well as the market itself working as an agent of powerful institutions of the advanced regions. An attempt is made in the rest of this chapter to identify the policies which were responsible for the slowdown in the respective real economies of these three countries.

Structural Changes in Economies and the Rise of Finance to Dominance

As pointed out in the previous chapter, the relative quantitative weight of finance relates to the changing contributions to GDP by different sectors in an economy.[2] The services sector, which contains transactions in high-value financial assets as a major component, has consistently provided more than half the share of GDP in most countries. The pattern gets reflected in the declining shares of the remaining sectors, especially of industry. In Argentina, the share of industry has been consistently less than 20 per cent since 2015. The decline in general of sectors other than services has been operative since the global recession under the GFC.

The services sector, with high-value financial transactions as a major component, went hand-in-hand with large shares from finance to GDP. The 'quantitative weight' of finance as above acquired some 'qualitative' support from a socio-political scenario which facilitated the ascent of finance to a level of dominance in the economy. The process led to changes affecting the balance of power relations – which in turn led to further changes in the same direction. This points to a *circuitous link* between socio-political and economic forces on the one hand, and the weight or power relations between different sectors on the other – with both continuing to shape the dynamics of structural changes within economies. More of this pattern will be analysed later, in chapter 5.

We provide in Figure 3.5 below, the sector-wise shares to the respective GDP of the three EMEs of Latin America between 2011 and 2023. As pointed out in chapter 2, structural changes in economies and the related power (or weight) of individual sectors have a link to the relative profitability of activities between different sectors. We mention here the economic force operating behind, which is considered in the literature as a *prime mover of changes* in an economy.[3] The dominance of finance which emerged in the process is a result of the quantitative weight (lent by expansions in the relative profitability of financial activities) and the qualitative support from the ruling state in the capital-receiving economies. One can witness the qualitative support from the new legal as well as institutional changes currently taking place in those countries.

FIGURE 3.5 *Sector shares of GDP in Argentina, Brazil and Mexico, 2011–23* in percentages

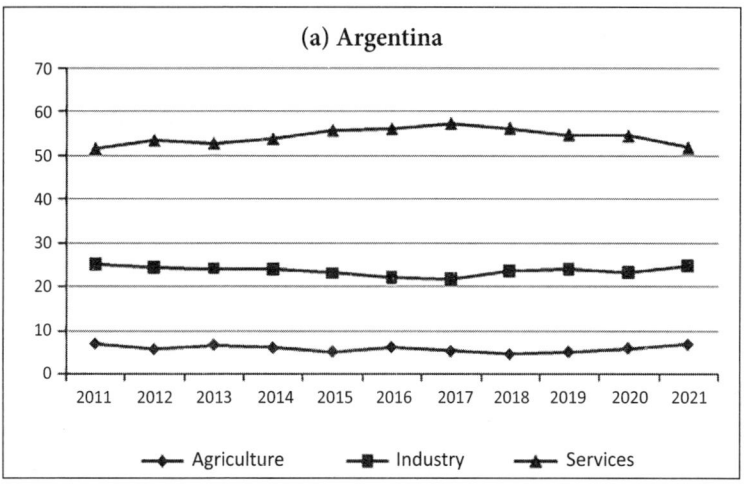

Source: https://www.statista.com/statistics/314743/share-of-economic-sectors-in-the-gdp-in-argentina/

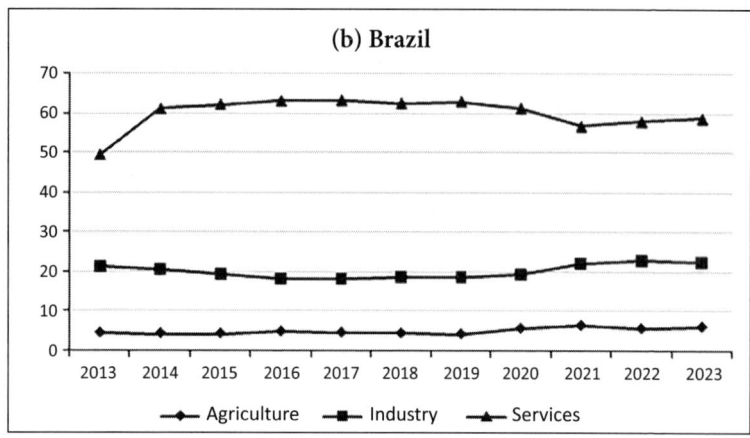

Source: As in Figure 3.5(a).

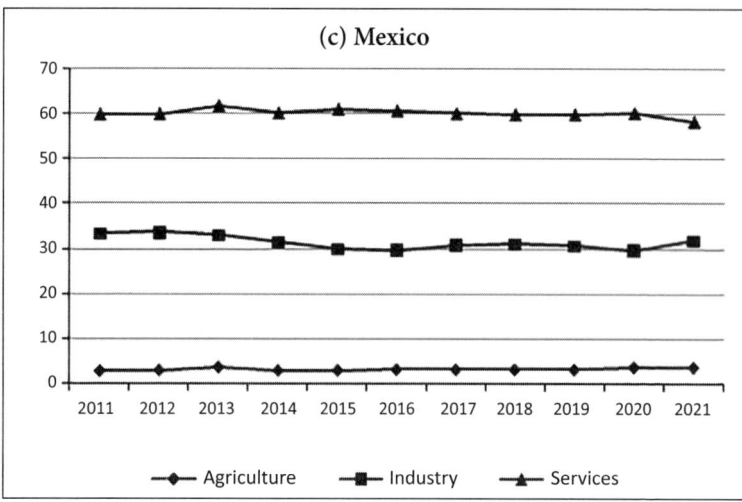

Source: As in Figure 3.5(a).

As structural changes continue, the underlying *path* or the *traverse* is determined by the *web of interdependence* between sectors within the economy – subject to the given resource and technological status.[4] The form of interdependence has already been described in chapter 2.[5] As mentioned there, the outcome of such changes could take different turns with conflicting interests.

In such cases, the relative weights of individual sectors, often in the case of finance shaped and nurtured by socio-political and economic forces, become the *deciding factor* in determining the continuity of final outcome. However, as pointed out, such eventualities may not be sustainable, especially with the possibility that the interactions may not replicate and such continuity of the process is interrupted with conflicts in the interests of sectors.

Probabilities such as above, while recognized, may not deter finance from moving in directions which finally prove self-defeating in achieving the targets. Eventually a crisis may follow that jeopardizes smooth running of the system.[6]

ON THE SEQUENCE TO SUBORDINATION

Attempts made in this chapter to identify the subordinate status of Latin American EMEs indicate the underlying factors which led to such a situation. The sharp rise in net inflows of portfolio capital (since capital flows were deregulated under the wave of globalization) was largely responsible for what came up in the EMEs as well as in other developing countries as their subordinate status. As mentioned above, an unchallenged surveillance on the part of financial corporates and global financial markets worked to successfully monitor the direction as well as the content of economic policies in the subordinated host economies. One can identify, as a result, at least *three* issues relating to their impaired autonomy. These include: (1) the monetary-fiscal policy incorporating changes in the rates of interest and fiscal balance; (2) fixation of the exchange rate; and (3) the level of official exchange reserves.

As for monetary policy, reliance on liberalized capital flows from overseas and a managed exchange rate around some desired level can limit the options open to policymakers for fixing the domestic interest rates at the desired level. In particular, as free flows of overseas capital move up or down in the host country, those are likely to impact the exchange rate of the country's currency in the market. Policymakers, in such a situation, may attempt to manage the exchange rate by managing it at their 'desired' rate. This can be achieved by sterilizing the excess and adjusting the shortfall in capital flows with purchase/sales of foreign exchange against domestic currency. But since such actions add to (or may reduce) the credit supply in the economy, policymakers, by following the prescribed norms in neoliberal economics, target inflation by adjusting the domestic interest rates appropriately and/or adjusting the cash reserve ratios (CRRs) – actions which clearly violate autonomy in monetary policy. The impact also extends to fiscal restraint.

Countries with capital markets which are fully (or even partially) open also experience restraints in fixing their exchange rates, which is the second aspect of subordination mentioned above. While attempts to sterilize foreign currency flows may not always work in bringing back a suitable exchange rate, the result is often an overvalued currency which fails to suit the interests of the real economy. An overvalued rate is quite common in countries with excess inflows of overseas finance. The higher rate, however, may suit the interests of investors from overseas who can now gain better returns in terms of their own currencies. Also, appreciation of currency usually draws additional inflows of finance from abroad while reducing the competitive strength of domestic goods – a fact which is opposed to the interests of the real economy. The inability of countries to fix exchange rates which suit their domestic economies reflects a similar state of subordination.

We identify the third aspect of subordination prevailing in developing countries as situations in which their official reserves are much in excess of what is needed to settle the liquidity or transaction demands for settling external payments. Such tendencies reflect a *precautionary motive* on the part of the concerned governments to take care of capital flight and balance of payments difficulties in the face of unexpected attacks on their respective currencies. The precautionary motive relates to the low status of their non-convertible currencies in terms of the prevailing hierarchy of currencies in the global financial market. As mentioned in the literature, this has been described as a *quadrilemma*,[7] in addition to the trilemma faced by the same set of countries.

As for the official reserves which are held mostly in US dollars and often in US Treasury Bills, those bring back returns which are relatively low compared to returns elsewhere. The situation is indicative of a *reverse flow of capital* in the direction of the advanced countries, and on a compulsive basis.

There has been some analysis of the *effects of subordination on financialization*. The prevailing literature argues that *financialization emerges* in EMEs because of the '*subordinate nature of their integration* into the world economy'.[8] The situation results from the status of their currencies '*at the lower end of the (currency) hierarchy*'.[9] In terms of the above argument, it is the low status of non-convertible currencies which is responsible for their subordinated status and financialization.

Explanations of financialization in contexts of subordination as above,[10] in our view, do not reveal the precise implications of the subordinate status. The pointers of subordination in our analysis include lack of autonomy in choosing monetary-fiscal policy and exchange rates, along with precautionary levels of excess official reserves. These provide an identifiable account of the subordinated status of countries, which has not been discussed so far.

To supplement the above argument, we have drawn attention to the fact that liberalized capital flows, dominated by the short-run variety and managed by foreign institutional investors (FIIs), can have little impact on growth in the real economies of capital-importing countries. Further, remedial policies to address the problems of free and short-term capital flows, which include inflation-targeting, deprive the host economies of their inclination to follow an expansionary fiscal-monetary policy that could be of help to their stagnating economies.

Details are provided below, of the specific instances of subordination in the three individual EMEs of Latin America. In a previous study we had published about twenty years back,[11] we noticed a similar picture of a dependent status in debt-ridden countries in Latin America during the early 1980s, with a compulsion to follow the norms set by the IMF for structural adjustment loans.

The subordination experienced by EMEs of the developing region today is confronted with an unchallenged surveillance by the global financial market, providing implicit directions to the content of economic policies followed by those countries. The pattern of domination continues despite the negative impact of such policies on growth and equity in the real economy.

COUNTRY PERSPECTIVES: ARGENTINA

THE POLITICAL PANORAMA OF ECONOMIC CHANGES: EARLY YEARS OF INDEBTEDNESS

The trajectory of economic crisis in Argentina can be traced back to the *debt crisis* of the early 1980s when the country, under military rule, was going through an external payments crisis which resulted from a rise in interest rates abroad and a drop in the prices of commodities it exported.[12] Argentina had a sizeable amount of debt, largely from the recycled OPEC (Organization of the Petroleum Exporting Countries) surpluses with transnational banks, which lent overseas the oil surpluses parked by the OPEC countries during the 1970s.

Argentina's political regime moved back and forth over three decades – from the dictatorial government run by the military junta in the 1960s to the conservative civilian government under Peron in the early 1970s and then again to the dictatorial military regimes during 1976–83, which has been followed by a return of elected civilian governments since then.[13] By 1983, Alfonsin had come as president of the newly formed civilian government with majority support. Alfonsin, a left-of-centre ruler, was advised by the famous economist Raul Prebisch. However, populist movements against his relatively radical measures led to his overthrow in 1989 by the centre-right Peronist rival Carlos Menem, who ruled till 1999.

The changing political panorama had a major impact on official policies, both during the regime of Alfonsin and later under the Peronist regime of Menem. One can identify some of the changes in these policies as largely responsible for the stagnation as well as the state of subordination the country went through. One can mention here how Prebisch viewed the capital flows to the Latin American countries which included Argentina. According to him, the causes of the excess loans to Argentina lay in the conditions of the capital-exporting countries.[14]

ADOPTION OF NEOLIBERAL POLICIES

Austral Plan Comes with Austerity

The change from a military regime to a civilian government as President Alfonsin took over in 1983, despite its leftist leanings, introduced several austerity measures. One was the Austral Plan which initiated *freezing of wages and prices* along with a drastic *demonetization*. With this plan the austral, valued at 1,000 peso to one unit of austral, replaced the peso, the prevailing currency. Demonetization of the peso by the high-value austral made the exchange rate overvalued in terms of other currencies. This, along with high interest rates and liberalized financial flows to the country, were responsible for *carry trade* on the part of the elite who borrowed abroad at lower interest and exchange rates – to fetch gains from the high interest rates at home and overvalued exchange rate of the domestic currency. The consequence was obviously capital flight. Further, continuing uncertainty regarding future exchange rates and interest rates added to capital flights from the country. The Austral Plan, based on the neoliberal principles of austerity with inflation-targeting, was obviously unsuccessful in achieving its goals of bringing price stability.

The Austral Plan failed to curb rising prices during the Alfonso regime which lasted till 1989. Following the implementation of the neoliberal policies, Argentina's GDP growth rate fell to (−)6.95 per cent by 1985 and subsequently to (−)7.07 per cent in 1989 (see Figure 3.1).

One can mention here the large flows of credit which came from the transnational banks in the west to the developing countries in general, essentially out of the OPEC deposits in those banks during the 1970s. This has been marked as the entry of the capital-importing developing countries into international capital's financial circuits. Thus, by 1977, the launch of financial reforms in Argentina already placed finance in a hegemonic position over internal matters, including interest rates and wage rates.[15]

Initial resistance to IMF diktats, launched by the ruling government in Argentina, which included that under Alfonsin, gradually petered off as the crisis in the economy deepened. Notwithstanding the interim support from neighbouring countries to help control the crisis, the foreign banks started putting pressure on Argentina to conform to the dictates of the Fund. In the meantime, in March 1984, the crisis was sought to be defused with offers of bridge loans of $100 million each from the oil-producing countries and $50 million each from non-oil-producing neighbours. The gesture was considered[16] as one of solidarity from countries in the South.

However, in hindsight, it is less clear as to whether the move towards debt redress on the part of other countries in Latin America and some countries under OPEC was a gesture of *debtor solidarity*, especially on the eve of the Cartagena conference of

South American debtor countries in 1985, or whether it was simply a measure of compromise which was in the *interest of the creditor banks* for effectively bailing out Argentina, a badly indebted country.

Ironically, the collapse that came about in the debtors' cartel at Cartagena in 1985 almost coincided with the near-capitulation by Argentina, which had already accepted loans from the IMF in mid-1984 under stiff conditionality. In the meantime, continuing domestic hardships led to wide-ranging discontent with popular revolts in the country demanding an end to the wage-freeze and economic distress. In 1989, Alfonsin was overthrown by a junta led by the Peronist Carlos Menem.

For the conservative Peronists as well as for the elite in the country who came to power when Menem took over, IMF loans were welcome. The revival of conservative policies under Menem was made possible, to a large extent, by the ongoing resistance (of big banks and the vested financial lobby) to earlier proposals for nationalization of banks under Alfonsin.[17]

Peso Replaces Austral at par with the US Dollar: Convertibility Plan under Carlos Menem

Reforms under President Menem, who took over in 1989, continued till 1999. Of the two major changes introduced by him, the *first* was the Convertibility Plan (1991), which replaced the austral by re-introducing the peso and fixing its exchange rate at par with the US dollar. This was matched by his *second* reform which initiated full liberalization of the capital account. Both changes were consistent with the mainstream policies advocated under the Washington Consensus, which in turn were responsible for further worsening of the country's external account.

The Convertibility Plan also overvalued the exchange rate of the peso, the domestic currency, by having its exchange rate at par with the US dollar. Simultaneously, with expectations turning adverse for the peso, it generated an effective *dollarization* in

Argentina – enabling all private holdings of dollar transactions to reach the economy. The Convertibility Plan, by not conforming to purchasing power parity between the two countries, considerably eroded the competitive edge of exports from Argentina. The plan ended in 2001, when Menem's rule had already come to an end.

The reforms launched by Carlos Menem (during 1989–99) turned the Argentine peso to one of the most overvalued currencies in the world. While offering little incentive to exporters, those provided cushions to residents who had been freely building up dollar assets abroad as well as at home. It implied easy money for local elite using the free market, especially with capital account convertibility which by then was nearly complete.

The overvalued peso also inflated the debt burden when it came to debt-servicing in the local currency. As capital flights by resident Argentinians continued at a rapid pace, the pattern followed a 'bicycle' principle, with dollars borrowed abroad eventually finding their way to foreign banks as private deposits. It led to changes in the official reserves with a drop from $16 billion in 1994 to $10 billion in 2002.[18] The deterioration of conditions in the domestic economy led to riots which led Carlos Menem to resign in 1999.

Economic Crisis: Changing Presidential Regimes

Economic crisis in Argentina was followed by quick turnovers in the presidential office. Five presidents, beginning with President Rua of the Peronist party, came and left within less than a fortnight since December 2001. This reflected both a political and an economic turmoil, much of which had its origin in the economic policies of the earlier regimes. To provide an example of the impact, the official reserves held by the country fluctuated between renewed heights at $52 billion in 2010 and $66 billion in 2018, followed by lows at almost five-year intervals of each, touching $26 billion in 2015 and $23 million in 2021.

That the fluctuating short-term flows of portfolio capital were at work to bring changes in the stocks of official reserves held by the country is not difficult to ascertain. Thus, each of the turns in the reserves was preceded by positive or negative changes in these short-term flows which brought about the changes in stocks of official reserves. The sharp decline in the stock of reserves from $66 billion in 2018 to $23 billion in 2023 can be related to similar downturns in net flows of short-term capital, from $41.4 million of 2017 to a much-reduced flow of $9.49 million in 2018 and the negative sum at $5 million in 2019 (Figure 3.2). The sequence tells us about the *destabilizing role of short-term capital flows* for economies in general.

Debt Default 2001

Argentina under the Peronist Adolfo Rodriguez Saá, interim president for one week between 23 and 30 December 2001, defaulted $96 billion as external debt on 26 December 2001; this added to the severity of the country's external crisis. It also ended the convertibility of the peso.[19] Occasional attempts were made by other indebted Latin American countries to defy external authorities by putting up threats of default. Similar gestures on the part of Mexico in 1983 and Brazil a few times since the early 1980s were neutralized by the IMF and private banks with offers of supplementary loans under strict conditionality – largely to prevent possible disruptions in the financial market.

By the 1990s class alliances within Latin America were already subject to changes. The national bourgeoisie, which under Alfonsin and supported by Raul Prebisch was in favour of industrialization in protected home markets, was now more for alliances with foreign capital – both for finance and for imported technology as well as inputs, with a marked degree of import-dependence.

More Debt Defaults

There were *three* more debt defaults by Argentina over the next two decades ending in 2020.[20] While much of the defaulted sums were on sovereign debt, the stakes were also for the global banking industry as a whole with contagion effects across the interconnected banks; this was because the possible bankruptcy of a particular bank could affect the portfolios of other banks having transactions with each other. Such possibilities provoked the IMF, the multinational official agency, to offer debt redressal by disbursing loans to large debtors like Argentina. The sums were utilized to meet outstanding debt liabilities of the mega banks, the collapse of which was of serious consequence for the global financial system. The co-financing between debtor countries and large overseas banks did not leave any finance to meet the need of debt-ridden countries to revamp their real economies.

Peronist President Duhalde, despite Left Leanings, Failed to Achieve 'New Economy Measures'

In early 2002, Edwardo Duhalde, subscribing to left-of-centre politics in the country despite his Peronist background, took over as president. Duhalde apparently made an effort to save the economy under the banner of 'new economy measures'. These included the reintroduction of a dual exchange-rate system, and the conversion of all dollar assets and liabilities of banks back to pesos. There was even an effort to stem the outflow of US dollars from the country through a decree against dollar withdrawals of banks. The measures, however, were immediately met with stiff opposition, both by the elite and the working classes – many of them without jobs. Earlier, the Supreme Court of the country had also passed a judgment disapproving the measures.

The new economic policy of President Duhalde in effect was also an effort to win back the international financial community; especially the IMF and the transnational banks. But in effect, fiscal cuts and monetary tightening, as recommended by the Fund, were both in the air. [21]

Changes in policies under Duhalde also included a stiff 70 per cent depreciation of the peso[22] and even talk of official dollarization of the currency. With Duhalde's new economic policies the elite of Argentina who had enjoyed the so-called prosperity of the country in the past were waiting to feel good again, with renewed opportunities to launder money and to enjoy the best lifestyle that could be afforded. Alliances between the ruling oligarchy within the country, on the one hand, and international financial agencies, on the other, continued to prevail, thus undermining the sovereignty the nation could have asserted otherwise.

Duhalde's presidentship (2002–03) was followed by that of Néstor Kirchner (2003–07) and Cristina Fernández de Kirchner (2007–15), both Peronists, but apparently sharing less conservative positions on economic policies. Between the Duhalde and N. Kirchner regimes Argentina witnessed a temporary shift with *a modified stance* of the earlier policies while the right-wing Peronists tried to restrain the trend. The changes with moderation, however, remarkably impacted the GDP growth, which *moved up* from a negative rate of around (–)10.8 per cent in 2002 to (+)8.9 per cent by 2003 (Figure 3.1). Moreover, the negative impact of the global financial crisis on GDP growth, as expected, was followed by extreme volatility coupled with negative ranges over the next few years.

It needs to be noted here that the changes introduced even by the left-leaning Peronists *did not* bring about noticeable deviations in official policies from the neoliberal frame. Initiation of easy capital flows, an overvalued domestic currency as well as high interest rates – the last two in a failed bid to prevent capital flights – were supplemented by large official reserves of foreign currency under precautionary motives as tools, reflecting a *marked presence of subordination on official policies*. On the whole, official policies were in conformity with the standard neoliberal prescriptions advocated by advanced economies and international financial institutions (IFIs). The impact on the economy included stagnant growth rates of the GDP meeting with galloping inflation of 10.46 per cent in 2010 reaching 72.37 per cent by 2022.[23]

Recapture of the Presidency, followed by a Turn to the Left

Attempts to revamp the economy from what was viewed by Peronists as a state of disaster during the Duhalde regime, were however marred by rampant corruption, much of it led by the Kirchners themselves. According to unofficial estimates, the declared personal assets of Cristina Kirchner which stood at $2.3 million in 2003 shot up to more than $12 million by 2008.[24]

Economic policies however worsened for the country as Mauricio Macri (2015–19), a pro-market leader, was elected at the end of a long fourteen-year rule under the official Peronists. The economy slumped further after him, with the fluctuating GDP growth rate touching (–)8.6 per cent in 2020.

Political power shifted once again, to a left-of-centre party headed by Alberto Fernández during 2019–23, with the pandemic casting a shadow over much of their sought-after goals. Despite efforts to bring in tax reforms (opposed by the agriculture lobby) and other social benefits, negative GDP growth rates continued with volatility for some more time during his regime with a low of (–)8.6 per cent in 2020, followed by 10.4 per cent in 2021.

ARGENTINA DEFAULTS AGAIN, 2020–21

Argentina again defaulted a sum of $500 million in May 2020 while trying to restructure the outstanding $100 billion debt with private bond-holders, and also the $45 billion borrowed from the IMF by the previous Peronist president, Mauricio Macri. The country's default in 2000–01[25] was a result of its net portfolio inflows (liabilities) turning negative between 1999 and 2006. Annual flows of net direct investments were also tepid, failing to exceed $10 billion in most years after 2002. With capital flights fluctuating in an atmosphere of uncertainty, even official reserves held by the country were subject to volatility. However, the response was slightly favourable by 2021, with the pandemic tapering off and the GDP growth rate slowly moving up to 10.7 per cent by 2010.

The Dictatorial Regime of Javier Milei

Next came Javier Milei, a far-right candidate for the presidency who was elected in 2023. He introduced some draconian decrees and legislations including privatization, spending cuts by the state, scaling back of workers' rights and of the general right of the public to protest. In addition, there was a devaluation of the peso by more than 50 per cent against the dollar.[26] Monthly inflation in Argentina touched 25.5 per cent by the end of 2023, as compared to 12.8 per cent a month back. Annual inflation ending August 2024 shot up to a three-decade high of 236.72 per cent, while the poverty rate touched 40 per cent.[27] As for GDP growth rates, the high positive rate of 10.3 per cent in 2021 got eroded over the next three years, with a much lower rate of 4.9 per cent in 2022, followed by negative rates of (–)1.6 per cent in 2023 and (–)3.5 per cent in 2024.[28]

By the end of 2023, Argentina was faced with triple-digit inflation with net official reserves almost in the red (Figure 3.6).[29]

Figure 3.6 *Central bank policy interest rates in Argentina* per cent per annum

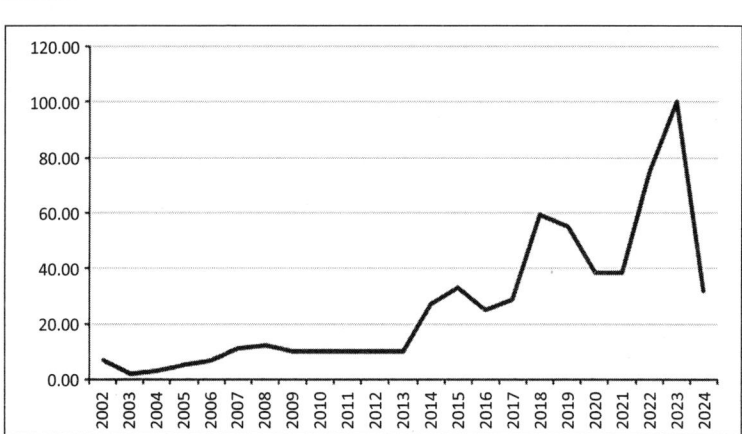

Source: International Monetary Fund (IMF), *International Financial Statistics*, https://legacydata.imf.org/

It came as a shock to the public to find Caputo, the finance minister of the newly elected Milei government, claiming that Argentina had an 'addiction' to fiscal deficits, taking place 113 times over the last 123 years. He also claimed, 'We're here to solve this problem at the root.'

Argentina's austerity programmes were reflected in the hikes the central bank policy rates had gone through, especially since 2013. The austerity package was much appraised by the IMF which had already granted $44 billion as loans to the country, of course with stringent conditionality and its related impact on the economy.[30]

Impact of Official Policies on GDP Growth and Balance of Payments: An Overview

The country, having often faced negative GDP growth rates over the last four decades since the debt crisis of the 1980s, settled into a state of deep depression. The downfall was precipitated by neoliberal economic policies which included up-trends in both interest rates and exchange rates as measures to control inflation as well as to attract foreign capital. While the neoliberal strategy did not work to help either stagnation in the GDP or external payments, the economy further worsened with the conditional structural adjustment loans from the IMF as the sole option to finance recurring deficits in external payments. With the economy on a downward path subject to volatility, pitching interest rates and exchange rates high were clearly against real expansion. Exports lacked competitiveness with exchange rates subject to up-valuation caused by at least two major currency realignments between the austral and the peso, intermittent calls for dollarization, and, finally, erratic flows of short-term capital – the latter making for parallel changes that were temporary in stocks of official reserves – often reaching precarious levels. All the above point to derogatory consequences of policies which were generally opted for by different regimes in Argentina run by diverse political parties.

Large debts were incurred by the country, subject to inflexible conditions in fifty or more prevailing bilateral investment treaties (BITs). Those led to further defaults in meeting services on bonds by July 2014.[31] The problems cumulated further by the end of the decade, leading Argentina to plead with international creditors for debt redressal, which finally led the overseas creditors accept, in August 2020, a 25 per cent cut in the value of bonds.[32]

However, while there was some downslide in the stock of reserves due to the unfavourable external payments faced by the country, excess reserves were generally held, even temporarily with short-term capital, as a precaution against possible crises (Figure 3.7).[33] This accumulation reflected the precautionary motive behind the holding of reserves, which in effect was allowing a *reverse transfer of financial resources* fetching rather low rates overseas – say, when invested in US treasury bills.

On the whole, the Argentinian economy, with negative growth rates recurring at frequent intervals, has been extremely unstable,

FIGURE 3.7 *Official reserves in Argentina* $ billions

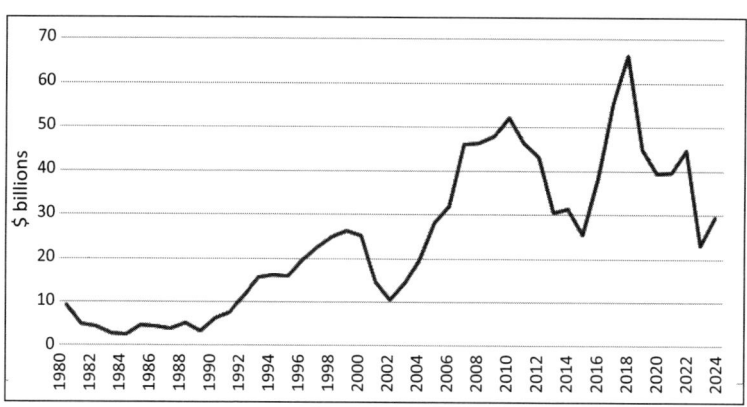

Source: International Monetary Fund (IMF), *International Financial Statistics*.

especially since the late 1970s. The situation can be explained by the country's less developed industrial sector, which has been one of the consequences of the structural changes in the economy with the dominance of finance under neoliberal economic policies.

Reinforcing of neoliberal policies and a push towards austerity came as a result of the Fund borrowings by Argentina under conditionality, which continued even under Duhalde despite his left-of-Peronist identity.[34] Argentina represents a classic case of missed opportunities for industrialization and stable GDP growth, that too despite having vast natural resources and energy sources, and being a leading food producer in the livestock industry. In our judgement, the potential of fast growth in the country which failed to materialize was a consequence of neoliberal policies chosen by successive governments, as already discussed above.

The GDP growth rate of Argentina turned out as *negative in twelve out of forty years* between 1982 and 2022, starting from the switchover to civilian rule under Alfonsin in 1983. This was matched by a deterioration in her balance of payments, largely as a result of the declining net flows of FDI, hardly touching $10 billion between 2000 and 2022. Argentina's experience compares

FIGURE 3.8 *Argentina: GDP, constant prices, per cent change*

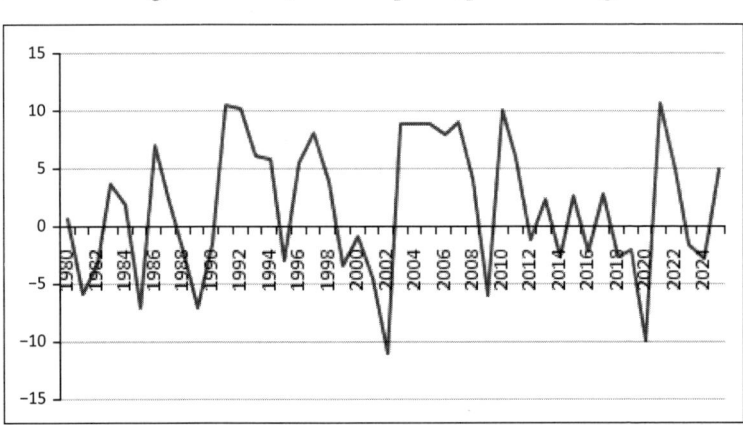

Source: As in Figure 3.1.

FIGURE 3.9 *Net portfolio inflows to Argentina*

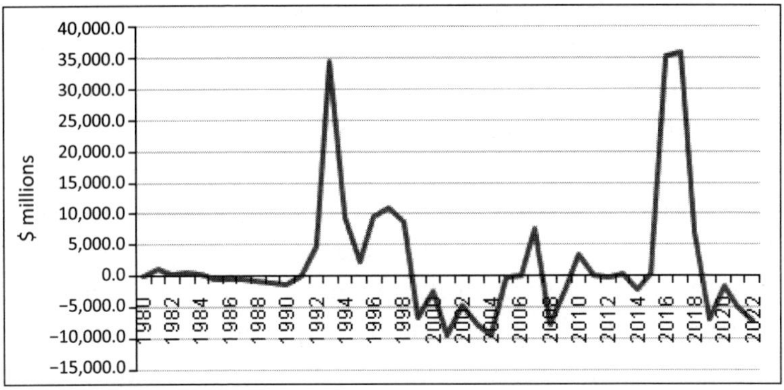

Source: International Monetary fund (IMF), *International Financial Statistics.*

poorly with the other two Latin American EMEs having much higher levels of net FDI flows, as observed from the average as well as peak levels of those flows over the same period (Figure 3.4). As for portfolio capital, the net inflows (liabilities) to Argentina fluctuated sharply between 1998 and 2022. The pattern of volatility in portfolio flows was similar for the other two EMEs we consider in this chapter, namely Brazil and Mexico.

Argentina also experienced a decline in its trade balance. All of the above led the official exchange reserves to tumble down to $39 billion in 2020, a steep decline from $66 billion in 2018. The quick reversal within a year to $45 billion in 2022 can possibly be explained by the access to loans from the IMF and/or other sources (Figure 3.7).

STRUCTURAL CHANGES AND THE GROWING POWER OF FINANCE

The structural changes that came up in Argentina with the deregulation of finance are reflected in the changing contributions of different sectors to the country's GDP. Currently, services account for more than one-half of the aggregate GDP in all three EMEs of Latin America (Figure 3.5). Given their high-value denominations, financial activities, as already mentioned, naturally carry a large weight as the major item of transactions within the services sector, thus providing the *quantitative* source for the strength of finance in the economy.

Neoliberal policies in Argentina, with their initial impact on deregulated financial flows, generated large flows of short-term finance from overseas. Simultaneously the market, subject to high degrees of uncertainty, generated demand for hedging instruments. Looking at the use of derivatives, we observe parallel movements between the flows of net derivative liabilities and net portfolio liabilities, both recorded as inflows – as can be seen between 2011 and 2019 in Argentina, years that precede the disruptions of the pandemic period and the Russia–Ukraine war. The similarity observed between the two series, as reflected in their respective log values, points to the correspondence between financial transactions as derivatives and short-term capital inflows which are used to finance the purchase of derivatives (Figure 3.10).

The large sweep of financialization, which included the prominence of derivatives in Argentina's financial market, also gets reflected in the profit share of banks in the country. These

FIGURE 3.10 *Derivatives and foreign portfolio investments (FPI) in Argentina*

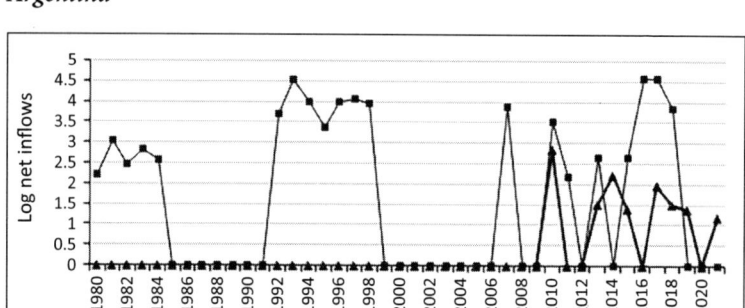

Source: As in Figure 3.1.

profit shares, which have been much larger as compared to profits in industry, by themselves indicate the prominent position of the financial sector in the economy. As calculated, the absolute value of profits earned by Argentine banks showed an upward trend, rising from a negative sum of (−)1250 thousand pesos in 2002 to (+)1000 thousand pesos in 2010 after the global financial crisis.[35] The record relating to profit shares was rather unimpressive for the non-financial sector including industry, which showed negative returns at (−)250 pesos in 2002 and a rise only to (+)100 pesos in 2006.[36]

As could be expected, employment generation in the financial sector was trivial, at 10 to 12 per cent of the aggregate employment in the country generated by the manufacturing sector during the pre-global financial crisis years between 1990 and 2007.[37] The share of finance to aggregate employment continued to be low. However, other services including tourism and transport made for a larger contribution of employment to the services sector, which was around 75 to 78 per cent of aggregate employment in the post-global financial crisis period between 2009 and 2019.

Impact of Structural Changes on the Economy

An explanation of the above changes can be arrived at by relating them to the impact of structural changes in general, as discussed earlier in chapter 2. Structural changes in Argentina followed a pattern similar to that in a large number of countries with services as a major contributing sector to the GDP. The country, possessing large tracts of fertile land for growing crops, the ability to rear livestock for exports, mines and sources of energy, had the potential to develop large-scale industries. However, its services sector, with a contribution of around 50 per cent or more to the GDP, offered very different possibilities, especially when industry contributed less than 30 per cent to the GDP.

Unlike the pattern in the other EMEs, tourism and transport were also major components of the services sector in Argentina, which also partially explains the contribution of services in aggregate employment, at around 75 to 78 per cent between 2009 and 2019.[38] This pattern has been broken, however, with the rather insignificant role played by high-value financial services in terms of their contribution to the real economy and to employment. And this goes on while finance enjoys dominance with its quantitative weight in the economy, complemented by support from the state in the form of institutional reforms that facilitate finance.

The continuation, in Argentina, of fiscal-monetary policies enforcing austerity in the domestic economy and the fixing of exchange rates at an overvalued level, as prescribed by mainstream monetarist doctrines, reflect the country's subservience to policies advocated by the advanced economies and their affiliate international financial institutions (IFIs). The market, operating on behalf of this overseas oligarchy, brings in the compulsion to follow its advocacy, with a potential threat to reverse capital flows in case of deviations.

Implementation of the advocated mainstream policies, along with the excess levels of official reserves maintained as precautionary measures, further reflect the subservient status of the country vis-à-vis the more powerful global partners in international exchange.

SUBORDINATION AND UNCRITICAL APPLICATION OF POLICIES

The present discussion on Argentina has sought to connect the dismal scene in the country's economy to official policies following neoliberal prescriptions. The package of policies started with deregulation of the economy and liberalization of finance. The measures brought opportunities for the financial sector to earn super-profits which were unpredented. These profit opportunities worked as a 'prime mover' of investments, expanding business in financial assets rather than to the real sector under 'financialization'.

As pointed out in Marxist literature, these earnings of surplusesare in the nature of 'fictitious capital' originating from 'circulation'. The income generated from these flows continue to be recycled within the financial sector for speculation, typically generating financial booms in the stagnant real economies.

Structural changes as they took place within the economy in Argentina brought about sector-wise realignments with finance, securing the maximum weight within the services sector. This provided one plank for the dominant role of finance over the economy. The other plank rested on political patronage extended to finance, with very clear endorsements from overseas governments, corporate finance and IFIs. None of the above were consistent with the basic principles of parliamentary democracies or civilian governments. One can predict unfortunate and perilous consequences for the Argentine economy in the years to come, if it continues as a subordinated neo-colony, subjected to surveillance and the dominance of finance.

COUNTRY PERSPECTIVES: BRAZIL

Deregulated Finance and the Economy

Official moves to encourage the entry of foreign capital started in Brazil during the *military regime,* between 1964 and 1985.[39] Previous to the upturn in the mid-1980s, similar upward spurts in growth rates of GDP prevailed during 1969–73 in Brazil, which was described in the media as a 'Brazilian miracle'.[40] Continuing with the facilitation of the entry of foreign capital, the civilian government which came to power in 1985 pitched high the domestic rates of interest for lending from around 2000.

With liberalized flows of overseas capital and with higher revenue from exports of commodities at rising prices, the investment climate in Brazil turned conducive at the end of a sluggish period, with improvements in the GDP by the mid-1980s. As for the exchange rate of the domestic currency, it was demonetized several times along with sharp appreciation. The above include, in more recent times, the change of 1,000 cruzeiros to 1 cruzado in 1986, followed by further similar changes till 1994.

The Brazilian currency, subjected to floating, depreciated moderately between 1993 and 2003. The depreciation provided a temporary cushion to deal with an impending balance of payments crisis. The country had a few years of moderately high growth rate till the beginning of the global financial crisis in 2008, with the pace backed by moderate industrialization. The change has been described as 'developmentalism' with 'approximations' to Keynesianism.[41] In effect, Brazil's temporary prosperity was helped by an alliance between the ruling state, and foreign as well as domestic investors, which worked well together to usher it in.

Structural Adjustment Loans from the IMF: Co-financing to Help Out US Banks

The civilian government led by President Sarney which took over in the mid-1980s in Brazil faced a rather grim situation with dramatic changes in the economy arising from the debt crisis of the early 1980s. While the country's external payments, as elsewhere in Latin America, was already in an adverse situation, further problems were created due to a reversal in commodity prices in international markets which also affected Brazil's major exports. Export earnings experiencing sharp declines and interest rates rising abroad due to the use of monetarist policies of the Regan–Thatcher variety to combat inflation resulted in deep trouble to Brazil's balance of external payments. The international context strengthened the neoliberal voices in countries like Brazil where those policies were implemented.[42] With industries relying heavily on imported inputs, the rise in global interest rates and the oil price hikes of the 1980s were further responsible for the country facing a severe balance of payments crisis.

A possible debt default by the major EMEs of Latin America in the early 1980s had posed a threat to the balance sheets of the major US banks. The likelihood of a contagion spreading to the financial sectors of the advanced economies led *mega-banks in the US to invoke the IMF*, the major IFI, to play an active role in remedying the global debt crisis by using what has been described as *co-financing*.[43] This entailed providing financial flows to the debt-ridden countries for meeting their debt liabilities to overseas creditor banks. While these loans, used for meeting borrower liabilities, were of no avail in providing resources to the borrowing economies, those involved a set of conditionalities which initiated structural adjustment policies in the debtor countries.

Tying loans to conditionalities was not acceptable to Jose Sarney, the civilian president of Brazil who came to power at the end of long military rule – lasting over twenty years between 1964 and 1985. To fix the problems in meeting external debt, Sarney stopped paying interest on loans exceeding $5–6 billion, which amounted to more than 2.5 per cent of Brazil's GDP at that time. Proposals were put forward for bank nationalization as well. Further, Sarney sought to swap 50 per cent of the loans for long-term bonds, which could reduce the debt liability. Finally, he launched an economic stabilization plan which changed the prevailing currency, the cruzeiro, to the new currency, cruzado. With 1,000 units of the cruzeiro equivalent to one unit of the cruzado, it implied a measure of demonetization with the goal of controlling inflation. In effect, both prices and exchange rates were sought to be controlled by introducing a fixed exchange rate for the cruzado at $13.88 and a total freeze on prices.[44]

Sarney's stabilization plan, including debt redressal, could not materialize, however, because of strong opposition from the domestic elite as well as from banks abroad. He soon withdrew its implementation process. Earlier than that, in 1985, similar attempts for a collective debt moratorium with the Cartagena declaration had failed, and Brazil had paid heavily, even bearing all the legal expenses.[45] A possible debt default on the part of the major EMEs of Latin America, which included Argentina as well, posed a major threat to the balance sheets of the mega US banks by the early 1980s, serving as a warning bell to the international financial community. In addition, the possibility of the contagion spreading to all financial businesses in the advanced economies led the major banks in the US to call upon the IMF to assume an active role in helping with the crisis faced by banks (in particular those from the US). As mentioned above, the IMF tried to intervene through *co-financing*, which, as mentioned earlier, was by providing finance to debt-ridden countries for meeting their debt liabilities to creditor banks overseas. We also noticed that while the IMF advanced these loans to meet borrower liabilities, the sums advanced were actually of no avail in providing financial support to borrowing economies. Instead the debtor countries had to meet a set of conditionalities tied to the structural adjustment loan (SAL) packages they received.

The situation described above ushered in the era of IMF-sponsored SAL imposing retrograde austerity measures upon loan-recipient nations. This also included the initiation of neoliberal monetarist policies in Brazil, having adverse effects for its economy. It began with the deregulation of financial markets to attain the goal of 'efficient markets' in the borrowing economies. The changed economic policies implemented in Brazil under structural adjustment brought in measures of austerity which further contracted the country's real economy.

However, the consequences of measures under the SAL did not deter the policymakers from their further implementation. The reason, to some extent, was the blind faith of the Brazilian authorities in policies prescribed from overseas, popularly known as the Washington Consensus; and the prevailing state of the country's subordination vis-à-vis the powerful, which included

FIGURE 3.11 *Domestic currency of Brazil per US dollar, period average*

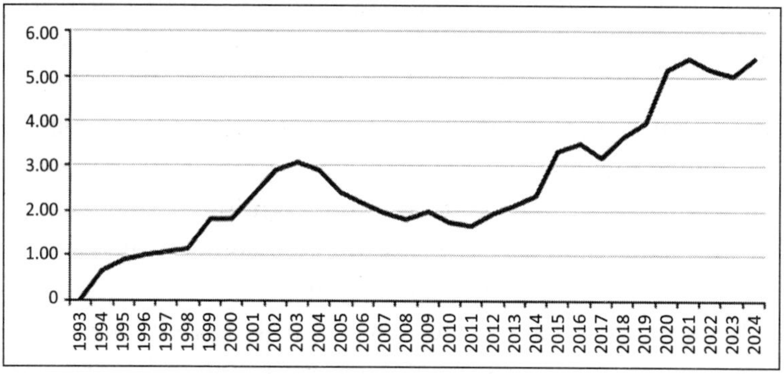

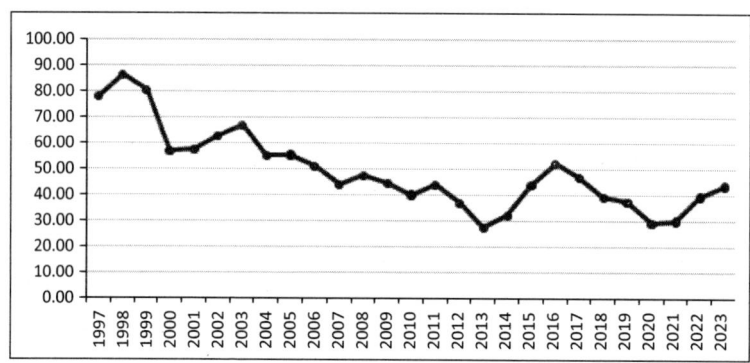

Source: International Monetary Fund (IMF), *International Financial Statistics*, https://legacydata.imf.org/

FIGURE 3.12 *Lending rate in Brazil, period average per anum*

Source: International Monetary Fund (IMF), *International Financial Statistics*.

overseas governments, trading and financial partners from abroad. It may be noted that even during the years of Brazil's prosperity and in the later years when it ended, official policies in Brazil relied heavily on financial orthodoxy and its related prescriptions of austerity.

Brazil had received large flows of capital during its days of high growth with industrialization. But the funds reaching the country were mostly utilized to meet debt liabilities as were due. Thus, with the borrowed funds amounting to $74 billion between 1974 and 1979, the sum used to meet debt liabilities was $56 billion and $7 billion accounted for capital flight, leaving only $11 billion for new investment.[46] Transnational corporations (TNCs), while having a lead role in the industrialization of the country, generated large external liabilities, mostly to meet the high import-intensity of products and to pay for their investment incomes, which was in addition to the leakages in capital flight.

The debt crisis that was faced by Brazil along with other Latin American countries including Argentina in the early 1980s led them to attempt a default. Brazil's move to default was hijacked by creditor banks wanting to avoid a run on themselves. New loans amounting to $2.8 million were offered by banks to prevent such defaults. A little later the IMF also came into action, using co-financing packaged with conditional loans.[47]

Civilian Government Continues with Monetarist Policies: The Real Plan 1994

Relying on monetarist prescriptions of inflation-targeting, Brazil frequently adjusted upwards the lending rate from around 2013. In addition, the exchange rate of the Brazilian currency appreciated considerably, largely to attract finance from overseas. The continuity in the adherence to monetarist policies obviously had a link to the subordinate status of Brazil's economy in relation to powerful partners overseas.

As for the exchange rate of the domestic currency, it was demonetized several times with sharp appreciations. This included the change of 1,000 cruzeiro as 1 cruzado in 1986, followed by further changes till 1994. Policies related to demonetization came up in Brazil with repeated substitutions of currencies by one another. On this Fernando Henrique Cardoso of the civilian government took resort (during his vice-presidency) to the Real Plan in July 1994, replacing the peso by an overvalued new currency, the Brazilian Real (BRL), which was linked to the US dollar at par.[48] This was a bid to control inflation which was around 100 per cent at that time. The measure was similar to the Austral Convertibility Plan at overvalued rates by Carlos Menem in Argentina. The move helped to tame inflation, with imported inputs to industrial output facing reduced local prices. The overvalued exchange rate also facilitated capital inflows, especially FDI, because of the rise in prices of financial assets in foreign currency.

However, as expected, the *overvalued exchange rate* led to current account deficits which, along with the high rates of interest and the fiscal squeeze (under austerity measures), were responsible for initiating a recession in the economy. Brazil experienced sharp declines in her GDP growth rates, from 5.33 per cent in 1994 to 0.33 per cent by 1998 (Figure 3.1).

Despite the negative impact on GDP, the Real Plan which kept the domestic currency afloat along with the dollar was allowed to continue – in particular as a safe bet for foreign investors by maintaining the value of their financial assets in Brazil in terms of the dollar. The net flows of FDI responded favourably by rising sharply, from $3.11 million in 1994 to $30.49 million in 2000.[49]

The changes mentioned above cannot dispute the fact that, on the whole, the Real Plan with the use of an overvalued exchange rate turned out to be a measure which went against the interests of the domestic economy. This was reflected in the stagnation of the economy which was consistently subject to GDP growth rates of less than 5 per cent in most years (Figure 3.1). The Real Plan for demonetization was probably one of the *compulsive and obligatory responsibilities which the ruling state of Brazil had to shoulder under subordination.*

President Cardoso, a sociologist subscribing to dependency theory, tried some *interim measures* such as imposing controls and taxes on capital inflows, mostly in a bid to curb the ongoing speculation in *carry-trade* by borrowing from abroad. These were aimed at controlling the large current account deficits and reversing the high interest rates, and as steps to address the declining GDP. The government also tried to stop capital outflows by enforcing a 'minimum maturity' requirement, which was described as 'sand in the wheel'.[50]

Unfortunately, the measures, even with clear deviations from the standard neoliberal manuals of orthodoxy, were not successful to remedy the situation.[51] With current account deficits widening further, Brazil could no longer continue with the overvalued Real and finally had to approach the IMF for a syndicated loan in 1998. The loan, seeking stabilization of the exchange rate,[52] made official policy return to orthodoxy by January 1999. The debt crisis faced by Brazil along with other Latin American countries in the 1980s induced them to again try default, as earlier attempted by Argentina.

Brazil has tried to default in recent times, a sum of $878 billion debt in 2023, amounting to 91 per cent of her current GDP.[53] The debt was largely from short-term borrowings, and interestingly, mostly owed to local investors who included the Brazilian elites. But despite such attempts, the default was not acceptable to the western banks and the IMF, probably also because their counterpart Brazilians were very close to the banks in the west. Following the prescriptions of monetarism, the Real now was to float in the market while inflation-targeting was continuing, pushing central bank lending interest rates up, reaching 15.75 per cent in 2000 and at 25 per cent in 2002 (Figure 3.12).[54] These were the highest rates at the time among other EMEs. In May 2020, Brazil's National Congress had enacted the Fiscal Responsibility Act with a formal legislation for fiscal tightening. It led to a primary surplus of $6.7 billion in the domestic budget.[55]

Policies such as above continued along with capital outflows even after Lula was re-elected in 2002, resulting in a large negative impact on the balance of payments of the country. To mitigate the impact of excess capital outflows on the exchange rate, use was made of treasury bonds (LFTs – *letras financeiras do tesouro* or treasury financing notes).[56] This measure, as discussed below, had a further impact on the balance sheets of banks in terms of related credit creation.

While orthodox policies continued to prevail during Lula's presidency (2003–10), the global financial crisis led the president to initiate some temporary policy reversals in order to address the sharp decline in GDP and rising capital outflows. Even the austere monetary policy was relaxed a bit by invoking stimulus packages through the Brazil Development Bank (BNDES – Banco Nacional de Desenvolvimento Econômico e Social) and other public sector banks. Meanwhile, changes announced in the US Fed interest rates under the quantitative expansion (QE) programme and its reversal had already affected the monetary policies of the EMEs with some adjustment issues.

Launch of QE by US Fed since 2008

Flows of capital in the direction of Brazil and other EMEs (as well as to other developing countries) went up when the US Fed launched the QE programme in 2008 and lowered the Federal Bank rate of interest in the market. The strategy of injecting liquidity into the market by purchasing bonds and other financial assets underwent a push in 2008 when the Fed responded to the global financial crisis with additional purchases of bonds. The rising bond prices pushed down the interest rates in the US market, which reached near-zero within a short time. As a consequence, capital started moving out to markets that were offering relatively higher interest rates, including countries like Brazil and other EMEs in different regions.

The Brazilian government responded to the inflationary impact of excess inflows of capital, mostly short-term, by instituting high domestic interest rates and fiscal prudence, as prescribed under monetarism. This brought about austerity with negative consequences for the country's real economy. Once again, the route taken by Brazil to address the potential inflationary consequences of the QE-led wave of capital inflows was to follow the path approved by the overseas lobby. Because of its subordinate status, Brazil was left with no other option. As we discuss below, this remained true under all successive regimes in Brazil – with Cardoso from 1995, followed by Lula elected for the first time, then Dilma Roussoff, Bolsonaro and finally Lula again, elected in 2023.

Central bank policy continued to be orthodox in Brazil. As a result, lending rates were pitched high in most years, moving up to 52.1 per cent in the post-QE year of 2016 and, at the end of a drop to 29.04 per cent in 2020, rising again to 42.6 per cent in 2023 (Figure 3.12). The taper tantrums in the US at the end of 2013 which came with the rise in Federal interest rates (to check rising domestic prices) were matched, in countries like Brazil, by high interest rates on a continuing basis. The high interest rate strategy and fiscal stringency that prevailed in Brazil were to control inflation as well as to attract funds from abroad. The strategy continued over different regimes with changing presidents, as mentioned above. Interest rates continued to be high in the country at the end of QE in 2013 as well, and even during the pandemic-related developments and the Russian war in Ukraine, to contain price rise and to also attract and retain foreign capital flows at those high rates.

The package of austerity-driven policies since 2003 were hardly conducive to the development of Brazil's economy, and were more in line with the Federal Reserve policies of the QE in the US economy. This once again confirms the *situation of subordination of developing countries like Brazil* that we highlight in the present volume.

President Lula's First Term, 2003–13

President Lula's first term in Brazil, coinciding with the QE in the US, saw rising inflows of capital to the country, where interest rates were higher. Appreciation of the exchange rate of the Real followed, from 3.08 (2003) to 1.67 (2011) per US dollar. Earlier than that, by the mid-1990s, the currency already had gone through a shock under the Real Plan of 1994 which brought in a considerable degree of exchange rate overvaluation.

The QE years in the US also witnessed sharp increases in net foreign direct investment inflows to Brazil, largely due to the relatively low rates of interest in the US (due to bond purchases by the Fed under QE). The trend in Brazil of high interest rates and appreciated exchange rates continued in the coming years, notwithstanding the stagnating economy which was experiencing further shortfalls in GDP between 2007 and 2009, closely related to the global financial crisis.

In the meantime, rising capital inflows to Brazil continued and liquidity expanded in the domestic market, causing additional concern about inflation among the official agencies. There was also concern about the appreciation of the exchange rate, and its consequences on trade and debt-related liabilities. As analysed, 'quantitative easing policies had strong spill-over effects on the Brazilian economy ... certainly benefiting household consumption but disruptive to manufacturing and real investment'.[57]

With the high interest rates providing a cushion to inflows of capital and appreciation of the Real considerably adding to the dollar-value of financial assets held by foreign stakeholders, expectations of further currency appreciation led to forward deals on the exchange rate of the economy. Interestingly, the forward rates of exchange between the Brazilian Real and the US dollar, as traded in formal exchanges, were controlling spot rates of exchange for the Real. This reflected the importance of speculation in the derivatives market.[58] One can also witness the ongoing outflows of derivative flows from Brazil, especially since the global financial crisis (2008). This points to the outflows of derivatives as measures to book profits in the face of upward movements of the Real.

The backdrop changed dramatically with announcements in March 2013 by the Fed that there would be no further liquidity injection under the QE. This started a new phase in the US currency market, described as 'taper tantrum', bringing a quick reversal of Fed policies. The new strategy adopted by the US Fed included control over inflation in its economy by using monetarist policies, which also implied an upward shift in the Fed rate of interest.

As pointed out earlier, the new strategy of raising interest rates, adopted by the US Fed at the end of the QE programme, was capable of affecting the direction of global flows of capital by directing these away from developing country financial markets. Its effect on Brazil also included, from 2013, reduced values of foreign direct investment as well as portfolios, which in turn affected its balance of payments. The response on the part of the Brazilian monetary authorities, once again, was to *push up* the interest rate further, to attract and retain capital flows to the domestic economy. These policies were implemented despite the contractionary effects they could have on the domestic economy. And many of them were linked to a loss of autonomy in framing policies.

FROM BOLSONARO (2016–22) TO LULA'S SECOND TERM (FROM 2023)

The Real, continued to depreciate from 2018 when Bolsonaro (2016–22) was in power and even later, when Lula returned for a second term as president in 2023.[59] The depreciated rate, impacted by the pandemic as well as the ongoing war in Europe and the Middle East, recorded a steep decline of the Real to 5.59 a dollar by 2021, from a little less than 2 Real to a dollar in 2010 (Figure 3.11).

On the whole, domestic economic policies in Brazil, as in most other EMEs, were subjected to austerity in recent times.

FIGURE 3.13 *Log values of net portfolio capital inflows and derivatives flows*

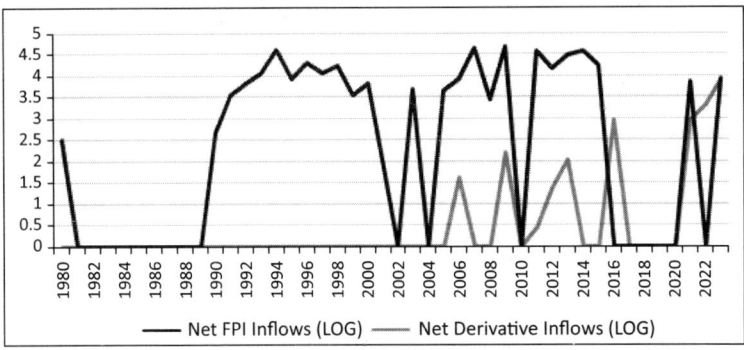

Source: As in Figure 3.1.

Those were also impacted by policy changes overseas, like the QE programme and its reversal, as well as by recent geopolitical developments such as the pandemic and the Russia–Ukraine war. The package of official policies in Brazil was in line with the accepted manuals of inflation-targeting under monetarism, which worked with total disregard to the interests of growth and employment in the domestic economy.

SECTOR-WISE SHARES TO BRAZIL'S GDP

Using an indirect method to measure the weight of finance in the economy, we can consider the following *two* aspects of changing financial activities in Brazil. *First*, the disproportionate rise in the capitalization of the Brazilian stock market (Bovespa) index, from 5384 in 1998 to 68461 in 2018 and higher still at 124423 in 2022.[60] The uptrend was combined with volatility of the index, especially in its lower ranges. The *second* indirect evidence relating to the active role of finance in the economy can be found in the parallel movements of net short-term capital inflows and the inflows of derivatives, indicating the magnitude as well as direction of capital inflows towards speculation-led financial activities. As can be observed from Figure 3.13, the rates of change in net inflows of short-term portfolio capital and derivatives, as indicated by their respective log values, moved parallely from 2005 to 2018. Finally, given that the value added by financial transactions tend to be much higher than those from remaining categories of transactions included as services, like transport, tourism, etc., it is but reasonable to expect that finance has a major presence in terms of its contribution to the services sector as well as to the GDP.

Downturn in GDP with Stagnation in Brazil's Real Economy

Brazil has gone through severe downturns in the real economy since the years of the global financial crisis, as indicated by the negative growth in 2009 and in later years between 2014–16 and 2019–20. As pointed out above, the continuing stagnation was combined with *structural changes* in the sector-wise composition of the GDP. It followed a pattern similar to that in other developing countries including EMEs – with the services sector contributing the major share of the GDP. In Brazil, 60 per cent or more of aggregate output on average was provided by the services sector as share to the GDP, but for a slight drop in 2021. The large share of services is linked to the relatively small shares of the other two sectors, namely industry and agriculture. Further, as in other countries, financial transactions within the services sector accounted for the major contribution to the GDP, a fact which goes with the growing significance of finance in the economy.[61]

However, as pointed out earlier, the quantitative significance and the related dominance or weight of the financial sector continued alongside stagnation in the majority of the EMEs. Policies to achieve further gains for finance had no agenda to reverse the pace of real stagnation. The pattern has been similar in Brazil, where the financial sector is the top performing activity and the GDP is on a downward spell.

We end this analysis of the Brazilian economy with some supporting facts from a comprehensive study of Brazil.[62] Pointing to de-industrialization in Brazil in terms of the declining shares of manufactures in aggregate exports from the country, and a decline in aggregate exports from 53 per cent of output in 2005 to 35 per cent by 2012, the study refers to the matching, subject to few deviations, of an appreciation of the Real between 2003 and 2011. It also draws attention to the effects of the appreciation of the Real in making labour cost more expensive in dollar terms while wages remained the same in local currency. As mentioned, 'profitability is affected, and the tendency to move towards rent, speculative real estate and financial activities ... which may be speculative, increases'.[63] The situation also reflects the spread of financialization and the overpowering role of finance in similar other countries in the global South.

In Brazil, large trade deficits prevailed in manufacturing units faced with declining exports. Of these, units manufacturing high-tech, mid-high-tech and mid-low-tech products, all had deficits in the trade balance, with a drop in the value exported and rising cost of intermediates. The exception was low-tech manufacture which displayed a surplus in its trade balance, and also better employment opportunities. However, aggregating the different categories of manufactures as above, the trade balance incurred large deficits in manufactures. The pattern, as pointed out in the study, 'reflects a process of de-industrialization, clubbed with financialization in the country, and deterioration of the GDP'.[64] Much of the under-performance in high-tech sectors can also be related to the digital divide prevailing under the current wave of web-based technology.

Brazil under Subordination

Brazil's experience with deregulated finance, as has been the case with the other two EMEs of Latin America we discuss in this chapter, confirms the pervasiveness of 'subordination' generally faced by similarly situated countries in the global South with liberalized inflows of capital. Our analysis draws attention to the lack of autonomy faced by these capital-importing countries in managing economic policies which could be in the interest of their domestic economy – for growth in the real sector as well as for overall stability. *The specific pattern of subordination faced by these countries relates to the restraints faced on the management of their exchange rates, on the rates of interest, on fiscal spending and even on the levels of official reserves.*

Instances as provided above for Brazil indicate situations where the country had to take major policy decisions that were of no benefit to the domestic economy. These include the attempts to demonetize and appreciate the exchange rate with the substitution of the cruzeiro by the cruzado on the part of President Sarney when he came to power with a civilian government in 1985. Similar steps were taken again in the demonetization of the peso by the Real in 1994 at an overvalued rate which was at par with the US dollar. Such steps, in effect, pushed down the plunging economy even further by bringing negative changes in the trade balance as well as the current account balance, and adding to a further decline in the GDP growth rate.

Consistent attempts by Brazil to pitch its exchange rate towards a dollar parity, along with the use of high interest rates to attract capital flows from overseas (especially during the QE period), often led to 'carry-trade' which brought profits on speculation-led activities in the financial sector. Brazil's exchange rate was consistently under *pressure from overseas to conform*: initially to the monetarist advocacy to liberalize flows of capital and float the currency even when the exchange rate was already overvalued with successive demonetization of the prevailing currency. From around 2003 to 2013, the exchange rate of the Brazilian Real was in effect determined by the moves of the US federal government on the QE. The consequences in Brazil included successive appreciations of the currency and high interest rates – to target the possible inflationary effects caused by excess capital inflows and also to attract foreign capital. Similar was the case after 2013 when the Fed decided to reverse its QE policies. The Fed rate of interest was pushed up to take care of what was viewed as signs of inflation in the US. Brazil in turn chose to maintain (and continue) with a high interest rate along with an overvalued exchange rate, in order to incentivize inflows of foreign capital and the returns on financial assets, as mentioned earlier. None of these changes in policies worked to the benefit of Brazil's domestic economy. Those only reaffirm our assessment of the underlying current of subordination in the country.

To conclude this discussion of Brazil, we draw attention to similar instances of continuing pressure experienced by other developing nations, from the league of creditor banks, corporate industry and international financial institutions, to deregulate financial markets and practice austerity by following neoliberal adjustment policies. The rise of the Regan–Thatcher brand of monetarism in the west during the early 1980s, which was remodelled as the Washington Consensus, has continued to cast its shadow on policies in the subordinated countries.

The Brazilian economy so far has continued to remain a playground for foreign capital flows, much of it comprising portfolio capital which is drawn to speculation in the market. In capital-importing countries in general, continuous attempts were made to keep the domestic financial market alive by making it attractive to foreign capital. In more recent times, the standstill over the pandemic as well as the geopolitical tensions related to the war in Europe have come up as major determining factors influencing the interest rates as well as the exchange rates in these countries. The changes provided little autonomy over policy decisions in their respective economies. And Brazil was one among those nations.

We need to mention here the latest move by US President Trump to reprimand Brazil for its involvement in the de-dollar initiative within the BRICS. This has entailed a 50 per cent tariff on Brazil's exports entering the USA. A similar move, with 50 per cent tariff on US imports from India, put these two countries in the same boat. This calls for wider collaboration with countries of the global South, resulting in trade diversification along with the use of local currencies rather than the US dollar.

We now proceed to discuss Mexico, the third largest EME in South America.

COUNTRY PERSPECTIVES: MEXICO

THE CONTEXT OF THE DEBT CRISIS

Mexico had accumulated a large debt by the end of the 1970s, largely with ample inflows of private credit advanced by foreign banks, mostly from the US. These banks were pushing[65] such loans out of the huge deposits of oil revenue in US dollars (petrodollars)[66] by the oil-rich OPEC of the Middle East.

The loans to Mexico during the 1970s were considered especially secure by its creditors because of the country's oil reserves. Capital flows to Mexico also became attractive to foreign investors because of the uptrend in the already overvalued exchange rate of the Mexican peso till the mid-1990s, making for high dollar value of financial assets held in peso.

DEBT CRISIS FACED BY MEXICO IN THE EARLY 1980S: FAILED AUSTERITY POLICIES AND SUBSERVIENT STATUS

Like Argentina and Brazil, Mexico also faced serious problems in servicing large outstanding debts falling due in the early 1980s. As with many other EMEs of Latin America, the problems that Mexico faced in the servicing of outstanding debts were caused by the drop in global crude prices (which affected Mexico more, given the country's large oil reserves) and the spike in interest

FIGURE 3.14 *Exchange rates of Mexican peso to US dollar: period average*

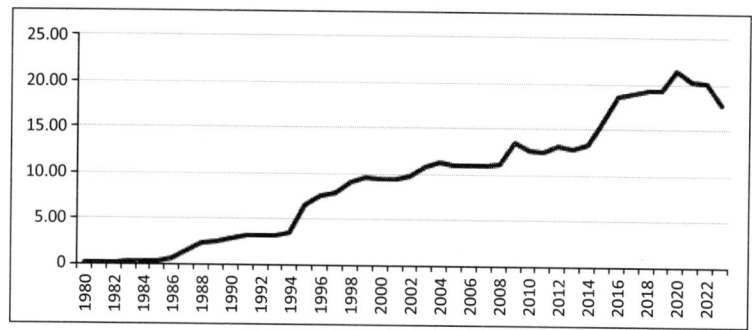

Source: International Monetary Fund (IMF), *International Financial Statistics*, https://tradingeconomics.com/mexico/inflation-cpi

FIGURE 3.15 *Mexico's central bank policy rate*

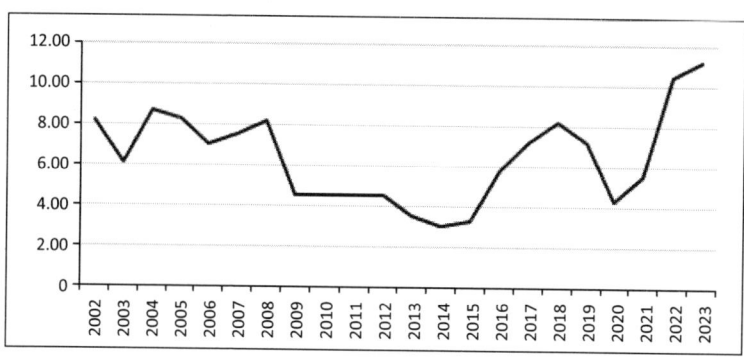

Source: International Monetary Fund (IMF), *International Financial Statistics*.

rates charged on loans from abroad, which was related to the use of monetarist policies in advanced economies. Mexico tried to adjust the exchange rate of the peso through successive rounds of depreciation between 1995 and 2020. This was both to improve the country's trade balance as well as to reverse ongoing capital fights from the country. In addition, the policy rate (bank rate) set by the central bank of Mexico went through upturns, with the same goal of attracting capital flows from abroad.

Policies such as above did not succeed, however, to have an upturn to the Mexican economy. On the trade front, the merchandise balance had been dropping steadily since the 1980s.[67] The balance slid down from $14.2 billion in 1980 to (–)$20.2 billion in 1995 and further to (–)$42.82 billion in 2022, except for a temporary reversal in 2020, probably due to a decline in performance of industry during the pandemic and a related drop in imported inputs.

The expected increases in capital inflows, in particular, were not achieved, largely due to a lack of confidence in the Mexican peso in the global currency market. Thus, long-term capital inflows failed to show much improvement in net FDI inflows to the country. It was only by 2012 that net flows of FDI to the country showed a perceptible upturn, a major explanation for which includes the altered geo-economic environment faced by Mexico under the North American Free Trade Agreement (NAFTA) which was signed in 1994 and later replaced by USMCA (United States–Mexico–Canada Agreement) which included free trade in both digital trade and e-commerce.[68] The pattern was very similar with flows of short-term portfolio capital, which, even with its typical volatilities, remained moderate till 2012 when upward spurts reached the flows to newer heights.

Unsuccessful Attempts to Default Followed by IMF Structural Adjustment Loans

Mexico attempted to form a *collective for debt moratorium* with Brazil and Argentina, but it did not succeed; similar attempts by Brazil and Argentina also failed. Thus defeated in its attempts for debt redressal, Mexico, like other EMEs, had no other option than to approach the IMF. This was followed by an offer of a structural adjustment loan (SAL) from the IMF which came with conditionalities. Mexico also availed bridge loans from the Bank for International Settlements (BIS) and from creditor governments including the US. As for the terms of refinancing loans, the interest rates offered were as high as 13 per cent, a rather high rate but which was usually common with such loans.[69]

The conditionalities linked to SAL included implementation of orthodox deregulation policies with pressure brought to implement austerity policies which Mexico was obliged to follow.[70] In effect, the neoliberal structural adjustment policies which started in Mexico with such measures around the time of the debt crisis came back, which also was in line with the Washington Consensus.

Austerity policies in Mexico began roughly in 1983 with the debt crisis and the connivance of the orthodoxy, which ushered in privatization, the dismantling of protection and cuts in public expenditure. By following this path Mexico fell victim to a subservient status vis-à-vis the international financial institutions as well, accepting their indoctrination relating to orthodox mainstream policies.[71]

The growth rates of the Mexican economy kept fluctuating around a declining trend, impacted by the structural adjustment programme of the IMF as the sole remedial measure to combat its debt problem. The GDP growth rate moved between 5.25 per cent (1990), (–)6.29 per cent (2009) and (–)8.65 per cent (2020), with severe instability all through the above decades. To provide an example of the destabilizing effects on the economy, Mexico's foreign debt, when re-negotiated in 1994, was matched by a sudden devaluation of the Mexican peso by almost 100 per cent. The impact with rising import prices and related effects pushed down GDP growth,[72] from 5.33 per cent in 1994 to (–)5.91 per cent in 1995 (Figure 3.1). The drop was also connected to the signing of NAFTA of which Mexico had been a member since 1994. The free market policies clearly were ineffective in terms of their ability to initiate growth.

Mexico Joins NAFTA (1994)

Difficulties in managing the economy, especially with the demonstrated failure of orthodox policies which were imposed on the economy in terms of the SAL, had prompted Mexico to join NAFTA by mid-1994. Creating a free trade zone between Mexico, Canada and the US, it led to a removal of all tariffs and quotas by Mexico on imports from Canada and the US.

Attention may be drawn here to the fact that the US has been Mexico's largest trade partner over a considerable time, with a very large proportion of Mexican exports, about 90 per cent, being shipped to the US by 2011.[73] In 2016, Mexico's exports to the US and Canada (its NAFTA partners) respectively comprised 80.1 per cent and 11.1 per cent,[74] which in effect implied a heavy dependence on North American markets. The share of the US alone in Mexico's exports has continued to be high, reaching 78.1 per cent in 2021.[75] The high share continued despite global trade disruptions related to the pandemic and the war in Ukraine during 2020 and 2021.

As indicated by what is narrated above, Mexico's economy developed an intense and dependent relation vis-à-vis the US economy. Consequences above for Mexico were rather severe during the 2008 US financial crisis, which hit Mexico more than any other Latin American country. In more recent times, the emergence of China as a major US trading partner has to some extent reduced further growth of Mexican exports to the US. It thus appears that developments in the US, which relate not only to the economy but no less to the political scene (including the recent change in regime under Donald Trump), were having a profound effect on the present as well as the future of the Mexican economy; this also takes away the possibilities, if any, of Mexico following a path of autonomous development. The dependence of Mexico's exports on the US market has currently backfired with Trump initially targeting 25 per cent (or above) tariff duties on all

US imports from Mexico, and in addition, another 25 per cent on automobiles and components imported from Mexico and other countries. Trump, however, brings in surprises with changes in his strategy with trade, tariffs and geopolitics, leaving the future completely unknown. As we point out below, use of the Mexican border by US corporates to outsource production there has been responsible for large-scale exports by those units back to the US. The recent tariff negotiations under threat by Trump may affect the business of those *maquiladora* units as well, further affecting aggregate employment and output in Mexico.[76]

As in the rest of the world, Mexico's economy has also been affected by a couple of major global shocks in recent years. Those include the pandemic attack of 2020 and the Russia–Ukraine war, followed by the Israel–Palestine–Iran war, all happening simultaneously. Growing geopolitical tensions have generated tendencies among foreign direct investors to relocate and concentrate within blocs of aligned countries.[77] All this affected, in particular, the global value chains for processing activities in Mexico. As estimated by the United Nations Conference on Trade and Development (UNCTAD), the expected output gap for Mexico was around (−)5.8 per cent during 2022.[78]

The fact remains that the growth rate of the Mexican economy has been extremely volatile, with the fluctuations in its rate of GDP growth continuing over time. It must be noted that Mexico's annual GDP growth in most years since the early 1960s failed to touch even 5 per cent, and its average annual growth rate between 1980 and 2022 has been just above a nominal 2 per cent (Figure 3.1).[79]

FDI Flows to Maquiladoras:
Subcontracting with Cheap Labour

High interest rates, along with the attraction of cheap labour used in subcontracting in the *maquiladoras*,[80] worked well to draw FDI flows in the direction of Mexico.

As has been pointed out, the flows of overseas capital to the EMEs of Latin America often moved in the direction of non-financial corporates. These flows, providing excess liquidity, spilled over to financial assets with hikes in their market prices. It is argued that while the high prices of those assets worked well as collateral against fresh loans, further problems were created when it came to the servicing of those loans, especially with the prevailing high interest rates in Mexico.[81]

FAILURE OF OPEN ECONOMY POLICY IN MEXICO: SOME FURTHER ISSUES

In an open economy drive launched by Mexico, there was an important emphasis on export promotion to help the balance of payments crisis. The strategy, however, led to a *bifurcated pattern* in the economy, with manufacturing units producing high-tech export-oriented products operating within an 'enclave', and having hardly any impact on industries producing for local usage. Thus, there were no *backward or forward linkages* between the exporting and the non-trade (or domestic) sector. In addition, the exporting units operated as processing sectors (or GVCs) that needed large net imports of medium-tech (especially medium–high) imports.[82]

Export units in Mexico, run by foreign enterprises and reliant on cheap labour and imported components, were however largely processing and exporting consumable products which were mostly exported for the US public. But in effect, these export earnings were used up to pay for remittances by the *maquiladora* units themselves.[83] Production by large numbers of those units at the Mexican border was obviously delivering handsome profits to the parent companies located in the US. Interestingly, the trade balance of individual units at the border often turned out to be negative, having a negative impact on GDP growth in Mexico by contracting aggregate demand.

The disruptions in global value chains during the pandemic in

2000 and the following years significantly affected the production as well as exports of processing units in Mexico, most of which were heavily dependent on these value chains. This has been responsible for the increased unemployment and related decline in aggregate demand which have arisen in the country in recent times. Aspects such as above precipitated an impending economic depression with the prospect of an L-shaped recovery, as has been pointed out by the UNCTAD as well as by other researchers like Pierre Salama. As for the strategy of export promotion launched by Mexico, while exports rose as *ratios* of the GDP to 28 per cent on average during 2000–12, this rise did not help in arresting the stagnating GDP growth rate from touching negative rates in several years since the 1980s, and achieving higher rates at 5.83 per cent for *the first time* in 2021 (Figure 3.1). A major explanation for the low GDP growth rate in the country could be the high import-intensity, both of exportable products and of items demanded within the domestic economy. In effect, the trade balance had to be in the negative, and that too despite the rise in exports which could add very little as net additional demand to the economy.

Finally, the ratio of investment or gross capital formation (GCF) to GDP in Mexico was much lower than the ratio of exports to GDP. Hence, the contribution of exports to GCF was *less* than its contribution to the GDP. The economy, as a result, encountered a process of de-industrialization, with exports in recent years consisting of raw materials, in addition to manufactures with high import content.[84]

DOMESTIC ECONOMIC POLICIES IN MEXICO: IMPACTED BY THE QE IN THE US

As mentioned above, domestic economic policies in Mexico were also influenced by the QE policy in the US (2003–13), which was launched to counter the spillover effects of the recession in the US under the GFC. Measures adopted in Mexico (as in Argentina and Brazil) made use of monetarist remedies, including currency depreciation. In addition, the policy rate of interest set by the central bank of Mexico was made to move in an upward direction, reaching 8 per cent and above during the QE years with temporary downturns. The rate of interest shot up again in 2018, crossing 8 per cent (even at the end of the QE in 2013) and touching 11.25 per cent by 2023, a year exposed to several geopolitical concerns (Figure 3.15).

Mexico, along with other developing and emerging economies, faced constraints regarding the choice of autonomous monetary and fiscal policies as a result of the QE policy implemented by the US between 2008 and 2013. To repeat, the escalation of interest rates by the US Fed which started at the end of the QE in 2013 had repercussions on the capital-importing economies including Mexico. In most of those countries the interest rate was tightened upwards in response, largely to avoid capital flights from within.

Denied monetary autonomy, these EMEs also tightened fiscal policies – along with implementation of overvalued exchange rates. As mentioned, these measures were to attract foreign finance, especially short-term flows for speculation – to the detriment of the respective domestic economies.[85] Even the reversal of the QE (or 'taper tantrums') was problematic for the capital-importing countries in the developing region, given that these countries were *not inclined to deviate from the ongoing inflation-targeting strategy*, of continuing with stiff interest rates. In Mexico, controls over prices were tightened further with the country's entry into NAFTA in 1994. Closeness to the US economy instilled a 'fear' of some pressure of floating its currency, and the only option left was to monitor prices with inflation-targeting.[86]

As for capital flows, net inflows of FDI continued to reach Mexico from 2013, even when the QE was replaced by a high-interest regime in the US led by the Fed. Portfolios, as mentioned, followed with volatility.

STRUCTURAL CHANGES WITH SECTOR-WISE CONTRIBUTIONS TO THE GDP OF MEXICO: RISE OF FINANCE TO DOMINANCE

In Mexico, as in the other EMEs, the contribution of the services sector to GDP has been as high as 60 per cent or more since the last decade. Some of the transactions labelled as services can be identified in the processing activities outsourced from domestic industry.[87] Other than these, there are some other important activities of the services sector that have had a rapid turnover in recent times, of which finance is the major one. The pattern is reflected in the rapid circulation of short-term capital flows from abroad. As in Brazil or Argentina, net inflows of short-term (portfolio) capital have been moving parallel to net flows of derivatives since 2014. This can be captured from Figure 3.16 by comparing the movements in the log values of respective flows.

As for the rising activities in the financial sector which was backed by demand for short-term financial assets, the major explanation includes the *relative* profitability of the assets held in the financial sector. The drive, as we pointed out earlier, works as the *prime mover* of changes that take place in the pattern of

FIGURE 3.16 *Mexico: net short-term capital flows and net derivative flows*

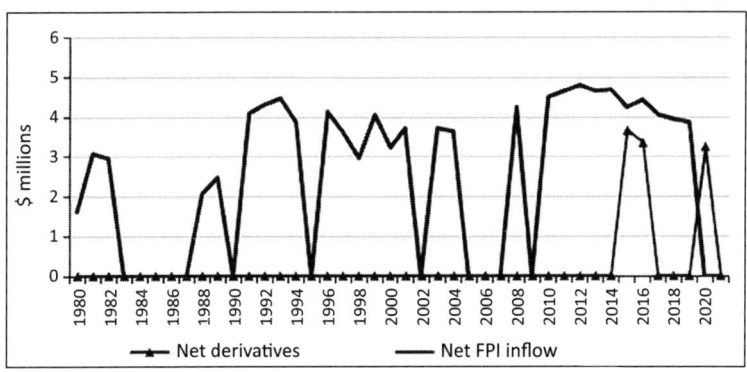

Source: International Monetary Fund (IMF), *International Financial Statistics*.

the structural dynamics in countries.[88] The argument also runs parallel to the analysis of *financialization* which results on account of the relative profitability of financial assets in the market.[89]

Flows of FDI reaching non-financial corporations (NFCs) of Mexico were, as mentioned above, often in excess of their immediate need, and money flowed out from the corporates to the purchase of financial assets that were mostly short-term. The pattern is similar to what we observe in other EMEs including India.[90]

We now consider the relative shares of different sectors in the Mexican economy to the country's GDP. As mentioned above, services consistently accounted for 60 per cent of Mexico's GDP. Using the same logic as we used earlier for the other two EMEs, we can observe that the share of finance to Mexico's GDP was proportionately large, providing the financial sector with its *quantitative weight* in the economy. This was supplemented by facilitation from the state as well as the society under capitalism, rendering the *qualitative aspects* of the weight of finance, which made for its dominance and power over the economy as a whole.

As for industry, with a share of around 30 per cent or less of Mexico's GDP since 1994, the proportion of the processing activities, taken separately, has been linked to the dependence of the country on the US market – in particular, after the annunciation of the NAFTA in 1994. Between processing and other activities, about 80 per cent of Mexico's aggregate exports were reaching the US alone in 2021 and later years. Industrial activities in Mexico, even before it joined NAFTA, were largely concentrated in processing on behalf of US companies. And these units excluded the capital-intensive activities of domestic corporations.

Finally, the small share of industry relative to services can also be attributed to the 'splintering' of the global value chains – set up originally under globalization – which was further aggravated during the current decade by disruptions under the pandemic

FIGURE 3.17 *Mexico: sector-wise contribution to GDP*

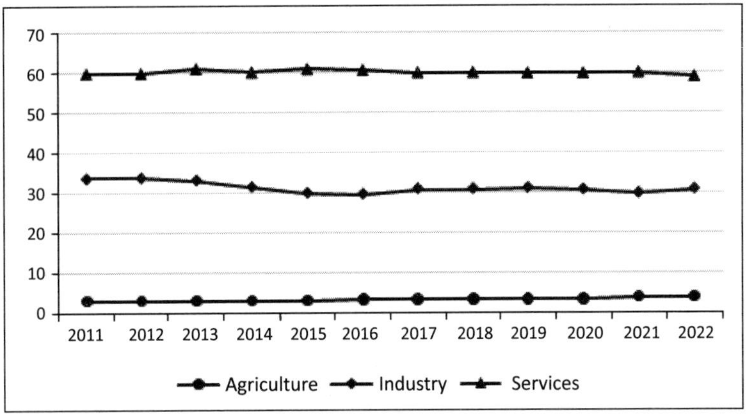

Source: https://www.statista.com/statistics/275420/distribution-of-
gross-domestic-product-gdp-across-economic-sectors-in-mexico/#:~:text
=In%202021%2C%20agriculture%20contributed%20around,further
%20information%2C%20see%20Mexico's%20GDP.

and the ongoing war in Europe and the Middle East. While all
this does not necessarily reflect the actual share of the industrial
sector relative to services (which includes the major share of
finance), it may explain the drop in absolute value of industrial
output in recent years.

The stagnation in Mexico's GDP can also be related to the
declining ratio of gross capital formation to GDP, which has been
in the range of 20–21 per cent since 2010.[91] As mentioned above,
the contribution of exports to gross capital formation has also
been rather low. The low growth rate of GDP thus gets reflected
in the modest contribution of the industrial sector to Mexico's
GDP, hovering around 30 per cent or less over the last decade.

As in the rest of the EMEs of Latin America, finance started
getting an upper hand in Mexico by the 1990s when capital flows
were liberalized. Additional support came from the US financial
lobby which had an interest in Mexican processing units in the
border areas.

The country experienced, from the mid-1990s, a boom in

inflows of FDIs, matched by portfolio capital, with the upward trends subject to volatility. The boom in capital inflows to Mexico was matched by a climate of high risk and uncertainty in the financial market, largely generated by short-term flows. One can point to the range of volatility in net portfolio flows, moving between zero million in 2002 and $74.7 billion in 2012. There was a drastic decline, however, of net portfolio flows over the next few years – with the pandemic and the Ukraine war, responsible for large negative inflows, reaching (−)$18.8 million by 2021.

In contrast to the volatile flows of portfolios, net FDI flows to Mexico continued mostly as positive values and at moderate levels. As mentioned above, the sustained flows of FDI were virtually linked to the outsourcing of production by the *maquiladoras*, effectively US companies, processing at cheaper cost along the Mexican border.

It can be gathered from the above that Mexico, like the other EMEs, faced a domination of finance, reflected in the large contribution of services to GDP (of which finance was a major component). The *quantitative* significance of financial activities in terms of its relatively large share to GDP went with the *qualitative* aspects of institutional support, especially through the NAFTA-related alliances between the state and the financial sector. The latter made for the facilitation of finance in the market by changing financial institutions like banks and stock markets which made for 'financialization', and making investments in financial assets relatively profitable as compared to those from assets backed by real activities.

MEXICO'S EXPORT POTENTIAL

Mexico's export potential and GDP growth rate thus seem to have been *overdetermined* by a combination of factors which include the following. *First*, while the share of exports in Mexico's GDP actually rose after NAFTA was implemented, from 31.87 per cent in 2014 to 41.05 per cent in 2021, the declining growth rates of the GDP since 2019 implied that exports contributed very little to GDP growth. Much of this was related to the *bifurcated* pattern of exporting units handled by the *maquiladoras*.

Second, the pattern of financial supremacy within Mexico, which went along with slow real growth of the real economy, was also linked to the pace of de-industrialization and the limited impact of net FDI flows in promoting industry – especially with the cluster of outsourcing units in the coastal areas of the country. As mentioned above, the FDI flows even caused some degree of overcapitalization for the non-financial corporations. The impact included rising financial activities of the large corporates on investments with speculation in short-term financial assets.

Finally, immigration policy in the US which was rather stringent vis-à-vis Mexican citizens had significant implications for remittance flows between the US and Mexico, the consequences of which provide further examples of subordination.

Furthermore, while Mexico became the third largest trading partner of the US, the share of Mexico in aggregate FDI flows from the US was only 0.6 per cent in 2018. But the fact remains that the sum had some significance for the *maquiladoras* – the clustered industrial units along the border which processed only outsourced orders of US corporates.[92]

The Subordinate Status of Mexico

We end this subsection on Mexico with a reference to the country's subordinate status vis-à-vis the state, as well as financial corporates and IFIs located in the USA and other advanced economies. The pattern was similar to what prevailed in Argentina and Brazil, as discussed earlier in this chapter. Mexico, moreover, was closely linked to USA, a major advanced country, especially after it joined the ratified NAFTA in 1994.

Structural changes in the Mexican economy, which included a rising share for the services sector and a declining contribution of industry to the GDP, worked together to contribute to stagnation. The pattern was in line with the rather small contribution of exports towards investments in the country, a fact that is explained by the import-intensity of exported products and the 'bifurcated' production pattern – negating the linkages (both backward and forward) between exports and the rest of the economy. This structural pattern continued, despite the fact that Mexico was in possession of multiple rich natural resources including crude oil.

While de-industrialization was continuing in Mexico, there was no industrial policy in the country which could arrest the downhill path the economy was going through. Nor could official policy be tuned to integrate the high and mid-tech export industries (often operated by the *maquiladoras*) with the remaining industrial units in the economy, largely medium or low-tech, which catered to the domestic market. Subordination of Mexico, generated by the changing structure of the economy, went along with the significance of the US economy for the country's trade and the pattern of FDI investments. The absence of an industrial policy to arrest bifurcation of the economy, between *maquiladora* processing units and units producing for the domestic economy, remained a major factor behind the continuing stagnation in the economy.

The steady depreciation of the Mexican peso, which started in the mid-1980s with the debt crisis, was slightly on an upward trend after the ratification of NAFTA in 1994. However, depreciation continued thereafter, as reflected in the rates of 15.85 pesos per dollar in 2015 to 18.66 pesos in 2016 and 21.49 pesos in 2020.[93] Despite offering competitive exchange rates with depreciation, Mexico was incapable of generating additional export demand to boost the trade balance and restoring aggregate demand. The country's trade opportunities were too closely linked to the US market, accounting for a share as large as 79.24 per cent of its aggregate exports to the world.[94] The restraint on possible expansion of exports which remained linked to US demand continued with stagnation of Mexico's economy. As for imports, the high import content even of the processing units allowed for no respite to generate improved trade balances. Also, since exports were not contributing much to new investments, their increase was not of much avail to arrest the ongoing tendencies of de-industrialization in the economy.

These developments explain how Mexico has been subject to a state of subordination from outside despite having all the potential for better outcomes.

IN CONCLUSION

We conclude this chapter on selected Latin American EMEs with some general remarks on their subordinate status while reflecting on similar situations faced by other developing countries. We relate their subordination as a consequence to their integration at unequal terms with global markets which was subject to the general wave of deregulation under globalization.[95]

We have discussed in this chapter the pattern of structural transformation in the three EMEs of South America, all of which have undergone a move *from the real economy to the financial sphere*. In hindsight, the contributing factor that brought about this major change was the proactive role of the state which prevails in most developing countries to emulate the neoliberal order of market-led efficiency. The state in these countries played a role in implementing inflation-targeting policies by using an austerity package with high interest rates and fiscal prudence, all of which proved detrimental to real expansion.[96] Deviations from the monetarist goal of inflation-targeting were often penalized by the market, by retarding investments from abroad, all with an adherence to and faith in the principles of efficient markets. In this, we highlight the role played by the market as an agent to procure and transfer benefits for overseas capital.

Going back to the early 1990s, the US government took the lead in instituting the universalization of banks. In effect this was more to facilitate the securitization of financial assets than for extending credit to the real sector. The new method of universal banking quickly spread, with the developing countries, much under obligation (and subordination) to overseas finance capital, playing an active role to promote the financial interests. While changes in banking practices were of no avail in revamping the stagnating real sector in most developing economies, the banks thereby actively promoted the derivative instruments for speculation in markets. This was done by banks financing the credit needed for transactions in derivatives and also by their active participation in the equities market, which was permitted under universal banking. The changes in dealings of derivatives had a close correspondence to changes in the flows of short-term capital. Given that the flows of short-term capital were often larger than the long-term FDIs, overseas capital flows had very little impact on the real economy of these countries, in terms of expansion of aggregate output and employment. Pressure as above to make finance profitable was brought to bear upon the state in developing countries (including EMEs) from externally determined forces led by big capital and transmitted through the agency of the market.

The transformations that took place in the three Latin American EMEs we have discussed here (as also in other developing economies) also relied on changes in the institutional set-up in those countries. Those have their origin in the alliances between the developing country state (in a subordinated capacity) and overseas governments along with their corporate agencies. This made it possible to change institutions within the developing countries, in a bid to enhance the transfers of surpluses via the financial market.

Some features of neoliberal policies in the two EMEs of Brazil and Argentina which can be recounted include the frequent demonetization of their currency with an overvalued rate of exchange and related capital flights with dollarization. For Mexico the status in terms of subordination was even more, having close links to the US economy which in effect was ruling the Mexican economy.

With liberalized capital flows, the large inflows – especially of short-term capital – to the host economies leave an impact with additions to official reserves which decline as short-term flows retreat under the threat of a deviation from liberalized policies. Much of these flows finally reach, via banks, agents in the market who use them for speculation in stock markets, real estate and other non-productive purposes.[97]

The state of subordination of these economies is evident in the compulsive application of neoliberal economic policies which have negative effects on the real economy. Finance, having achieved power with its dominance, continues to play a major role in the process of subordination which is continuing in these developing countries.

Notes

[1] Sen (2023a).
[2] See for analysis, Sen (2023b), pp. 468–73.
[3] Pasinetti (1981).
[4] Cardinale (2020).
[5] Also see for further analysis, Sen (2023b).
[6] Cardinale (2020).
[7] Aizenman (2013).
[8] Bonizzi, Kaltenbrunner and Powell (2020), p. 184; emphases added.
[9] Ibid., p. 178; emphasis added.
[10] See among others, Epstein (2005).
[11] Sen (2003), pp. 62–109.
[12] Stanley (2018).
[13] See for details, Sen (2003), pp. 162–68.
[14] Rapoport and Brenta (2021), p. 108.
[15] Ibid., p. 113.
[16] Sen (2003), pp. 161–66.
[17] Sen (2007b), pp. 25–26. See also, Bradford and Bernardo (1988).

[18] See https://data.worldbank.org/indicator/FI.RES.TOTL.CD?end=2 023&locations=AR&start=1960&view=chart, accessed 20 October 2023.

[19] Rapoport and Brenta (2021), pp. 120–21.

[20] See Fitzgerald and Gallup, eds (2023).

[21] Sen (2007b).

[22] See https://sg.finance.yahoo.com/news/argentina-2001-biggest-default-history-183426906.html; https://data.imf.org/regular. aspx?key=61545855, accessed 20 October 2024.

[23] Source: IMF; https://www.statista.com/statistics/316750/inflation-rate-in-argentina/, accessed 20 October 2024.

[24] See Roberts (2011).

[25] www.bloomberg.com/news/photo-essays/2019-09-11/.

[26] exchange-rates-org/usd-org

[27] 'Argentina Inflation Rate', available at https://www.inflationtool.com/ rates/argentina#:~:text=The%20current%20inflation%20rate%20 in%20Argentina%20is%20263.45%25%2C,the%20last%2012%20 months%20ending%20in%20July%202024, accessed 10 September 2024.

[28] See https://data.worldbank.org/indicator/NY.GDP.MKTP.KD.ZG? locations=AR, accessed 15 September 2024.

[29] See Rosario (2023).

[30] Sweney (2023).

[31] Stanley (2018), p. 106.

[32] See https://www.prnewswire.com/news-releases/argentina-exchange-bondholder-group-will-tender-nearly-5-billion-in-bonds-by-monday-august-24-301116306.html, accessed 15 September 2024.

[33] See https://www.estadisticasbcra.com/en/argentina_international_ reserves, accessed 15 September 2024.

[34] Sen (2003), pp. 163–66.

[35] Cibils and Allami (2013).

[36] Ibid.

[37] Ibid.

[38] Source: World Bank; https://www.statista.com/statistics/316858/ employment-by-economic-sector-in-argentina/#:~:text=The%20 statistic%20shows%20the%20distribution,percent%20in%20the%20 service%20sector, accessed 15 September 2024.

[39] Napolitano (2018).

[40] Baer (1976), pp. 3–22.

[41] Oliveira and Müller (2021).

[42] Ibid., p. 171.

[43] Sen (2003), pp. 158–62.

[44] Thayer Watkins, 'Jose Sarney, Hyperinflation and the Cruzado Plan in Brazil in the Late 1980s', https://www.sjsu.edu/faculty/watkins/cruzado.htm.

[45] Bradford and Bernardo (1988).

[46] Sen (2003), p. 160.

[47] Ibid.

[48] Leonardo (2018), p. 114.

[49] Ibid.

[50] Lucio, Pereira and Gomes (2020).

[51] Stanley (2018), p. 114.

[52] de Carvalho and de Souza (2010).

[53] See https://en.mercopress.com/2021/01/28/brazil-on-the-brink-of-financial-default-points-out-the-financial-times

[54] https://tradingeconomics.com/brazil/interest-rate.

[55] https://www.bcb.gov.br/en/monetarypolicy/realplan

[56] Stanley (2018), p. 118.

[57] Ibid., p. 123.

[58] Dodd and Griffith-Jones (2007). See for similar situation in India, Sen and Pal (2010).

[59] See https://data.worldbank.org/indicator/PA.NUS.FCRF?locations=BR, accessed 15 September 2024.

[60] See Brazil Stock Market (BOVESPA), 1988–2022, 2023 data, 2024 Forecast, https://tradingeconomics.com/brazil/stock-market.

[61] See Sen (2023b), pp. 468–73.

[62] Salama (2018).

[63] Ibid.

[64] Ibid., p. 24.

[65] Darity (1985).

[66] Amadeo (2022); Smolyar (2006); Petrodollars: Tracking the Flow and Investment of Oil Windfalls – Today vs. 1970's and 1980, http://web-docs.stern.nyu.edu/old_web/emplibrary/Leonid_Smolyar_honors_2006.pdf.

[67] 'Mexico Trade Balance 1960–2024', https://www.macrotrends.net/global-metrics/countries/MEX/mexico/trade-balance-deficit.

[68] ceccdata.com/en/indicator/mexico/tradebalance

[69] Sen (2003), pp. 166–67.

[70] Ibid.

[71] Lopez (2011).

[72] Basotti (2022), p. 7.

[73] López, Sanchez and Spanos (2011).

[74] See www.britannica.com/place/Mexico/Trade.

[75] Ibid.

[76] Sen (2025).

[77] See https://www.imf.org/en/Blogs/Articles/2023/04/05/fragmenting-foreign-direct-investment-hits-emerging-economies-hardes

[78] UNCTAD (2022), p. 16.

[79] Mexico Trade Balance 1960–2024, https://www.macrotrends.net/global-metrics/countries/MEX/mexico/trade-balance-deficit.

[80] *Maquiladora* indicates a factory in Mexico run by a foreign company which exports its products to that company's country of origin.

[81] Levy-Orlik and Bustamante-Torres, eds (2020). Also see Echenique-Romero (2021).

[82] Salama (2022), pp. 59–60.

[83] See also Sen (2024).

[84] Levy-Orlik and Bustamante-Torres (2021), p. 101.

[85] Sen (2024).

[86] Ball and Reyes (2004), pp. 49–69.

[87] Salama (2018), p. 17.

[88] For a more complete analysis of the point, see Sen (2023b), pp. 468–73. See for an analysis of the approach, Cardinale, Galbraith and Scazzieri (2024).

[89] Epstein, ed. (2005).

[90] See Sen and Dasgupta (2018) for similar investment behaviour on the part of the Indian NFCs.

[91] Baisotti (2022), p. 36.

[92] Aguila *et al.* (2012), pp. 151, 158.

[93] See also https://data.worldbank.org/indicator/PA.NUS.FCRF?locations=MX.

[94] 'Mexico Exports: By Country and Region 2020, https://wits.worldbank.org/CountryProfile/en/Country/MEX/Year/2020/TradeFlow/Export.

[95] Chakrabarti, Dhar and Dasgupta (2015); Sen (2007).

[96] Chandrasekhar and Ghosh (2002).

[97] Kaltenbrunner and Painceira (2018).

4

Subordinating Financialization in Emerging Market Economies (EMEs) of Asia

THE BACKGROUND

In contrast to the emerging market economies (EMEs) of Latin America, the Asian EMEs, which include India and China, have been following a *sequential path* in the successive stages of opening up their financial markets. The pace of reforms, less rapid during the initial stages in both countries, picked up rapidly over time. The trajectory of reforms in the two countries, however, was very different.

COUNTRY PERSPECTIVES: INDIA

POST-INDEPENDENCE REGIME OF A DEVELOPMENTAL STATE

At the end of the British colonial rule in 1947, India set a goal for itself to initiate a path of industrialization and self-reliance, and formulated policies which could achieve the desired changes. It relied on import-substituting industrialization and expansionary monetary-fiscal policies – both geared to generate demand-led growth in the domestic economy.

Such goals lent a developmental dimension to the country's economic policies. The strategy adopted during the early years of independence in 1947 also aimed for financial inclusion by arranging concessional loans from banks to poor households and small enterprises. Also, development banks were set up for promoting industrial expansion, while social sector expenditure in the fiscal budget was to provide concessionary benefits to those in need.

The first national government, formed in 1947 by the Indian National Congress, initiated expansionary economic policies alongside distributional goals. The economic policies implemented between the 1950s and early 1980s remained development-oriented even when other parties came to power in between, over brief intervals.

Of the major reforms in this era of the developmental state in post-independence India, one of the more important ones was the nationalization of banks, which took place in 1969. The measure empowered the central bank, the Reserve Bank of India (RBI), to mandate the sanctioning of priority credit, of up to 40 per cent of bank deposits. This credit was directed towards agriculture as well as small industry, with cheaper credit for very small advances below Rs 0.2 million. As for fiscal policy, emphasis was placed in the annual budget on social sector expenditure and public sector capital expenditure, both providing major supplementary tools for achieving the goals of development. In addition, attempts were made to institute development banks which operated very differently from the commercial banks.

CHANGING PERCEPTIONS AND POLICIES, 1977–91

One can identify a watershed moment in official deliberations as well as in polices implemented in the country between 1977 and 1991. In the year 1980, the Indian National Congress returned to power at the end of a brief period of rule by the Janata Party from 1977 to 1979. Indira Gandhi and, after her assassination, her son Rajiv Gandhi governed the country in succession between 1980 and 1989. By then, the priorities of the state had already shifted, especially under Rajiv Gandhi, from development *per se* to advancing technology, largely with foreign collaboration. Technological advances in R&D were undertaken by the major private firms in the country, which, however, was often on the back foot due to lack of funding from the government.[1] These were changes that preceded the wave of globalization which, in the early 1990s, touched most economies in the world.

Official policy in India took another turn between 1989 and 1991 under the Janata Dal (formed by merging various factions of the Janata Party) government, led by V.P. Singh. This was in continuation of the policies of the Janata Party which remained socially oriented. The V.P Singh government attempted to *redefine the norm of inclusion to cover social categories like caste*. While the status of individuals when defined in terms of caste often reflects their financial position, inclusion was not directly linked to financial status in the Janata Dal's notion as above.

The end of the Janata Dal rule in 1991 brought sharp policy changes initiated by the Congress party between 1991 and 1996, and later, during 2004–14. This was the era of *big economic reform* in India, which left behind the earlier developmental model with concerns over industrialization, growth and distribution. The Congress government that came to power in 1991, led by Prime Minister Narasimha Rao and the economist Manmohan Singh as Finance Minister, implemented wide-ranging deregulation policies in the economy, reversing most of the developmental policies that were still prevailing.

This direction of change along with a move for liberalization of the market continued undisturbed in the years that followed, even when the government was run by a party other than the Congress, namely the Bharatiya Janata Party (BJP), in 1996, 1998–2004 and currently in power since 2014. The same was the case with liberalization of the market when the Congress party came back to power between 2004 and 2014. By then, Manmohan Singh had taken over as prime minister. As mentioned above, the return of the BJP to power in 2014 has not changed the prevailing direction of the economic policies of liberalization.

Going back a little, the policy regime that was initiated in 1991 under the Congress government and which has continued since then under BJP rule, has generated deep inequities within the economy. Leaving behind the earlier norms relating to inclusive policies that were in accord with the developmental state, inequities at a social level have come up with the recent instances of a communal divide in the country. These changes have added further to the financial inequalities in the economy as well as the exclusionary social and economic policies.

We document below, the shifts in economic policies that have taken place since the opening up of liberalized markets in 1991.

The Sharp Turn in Economic Policy in 1991: From a Developmental State to Deregulated Markets

Among the drastic changes in India's economic policies initiated in 1991 by the government under the Indian National Congress, an immediate turn included the scrapping or dilution of most official regulations. This included removal of controls over external trade, and modification of controls over exchange rates and external payments. Other changes introduced in succession included removing priority credit from banks, initiation of marketized borrowings by the government to meet budget deficits, deregulation of interest rates, and easier access of foreign institutional investors (FIIs) to India's financial markets.[2] We discuss these successive changes and their impact in what follows.

As could be expected, the changes as mentioned above led to larger inflows of capital from abroad, the pace of which intensified with further relaxation of controls in the following years. A large part of these capital flows comprised short-term flows, motivated by the prospects of high profits on speculation in the liberalized markets under uncertainty. With FIIs permitted to enter India's stock markets in 1992, transactions increased significantly, as indicated by the rising figures of capitalization in the stock markets. Rising stock prices, subject to volatilities, fetched good returns to investors, especially as compared to those earned on physical assets in the real economy.[3] The flows were related to the ongoing phase of financialization in the economy.

One can mention here that the drive to induce capital inflows on the part of individual countries (including India) was essentially one that followed the wave of globalization, pushing forward the idea of integration of national markets with one another. One can also identify the *origin* of the move to liberalize markets to an *underlying allegiance as well as adherence* on the part of nation states to the neoliberal advocacy of 'efficient markets', which could only be achieved through liberalized markets, as mentioned in earlier chapters.

Looking back, we can identify *three* particular aspects of the new policies in the Indian economy under liberalization, which demand attention. *First*, the avoidance of inflation by using inflation-targeting. The tools in general target the fiscal and monetary policies of countries to implement cuts in fiscal expenditure (as well as deficits) and push up interest rates in order to curtail private expenditure, which in effect initiates austerity in the economy. Simultaneously the exchange rate is also kept overvalued, to attract flows of capital from abroad. *Second*, the practice to maintain foreign exchange reserves at levels often exceeding amounts adequate to meet transaction as well as liquidity requirements. Keeping excess reserves is mostly done by means of a precautionary move against sudden capital flights. *Third*, the meteoric rise to dominance and power of the financial sector with its quantitative turnover and qualitative support by the state in the economy. The pattern in India related to these three aspects is similar to that in many other developing economies, including the three Latin American countries discussed in chapter 3.

Inflation-targeting in India: Impact on Monetary-Fiscal Policy

Following the dictums of neoliberal economics, the realignment of economic policies in India in 1991 laid emphasis on inflation-targeting as a major goal. This had its origin in the monetarist principles of money and banking. In terms of monetarist theory, inflation turns disruptive to investment incentives, especially by dampening the profitability of financial assets in real terms. The tool used to control inflation, tried in India and elsewhere, following the quantity theory of money, was a restraint on money supply (M2) by closely monitoring money supply and credit through the banking system. Within a few years, restraint over the fiscal deficit was also considered necessary for limiting budgetary expenditure in the economy. This led to the enactment of the Fiscal Responsibility and Budget Management Act (FRBMA) under the ruling BJP government in India in 2003, when Atal Bihari Vajpayee was the prime minister. The initial limit set on the ratio of fiscal deficit to gross domestic product (GDP), at 3 per cent, had to move up, however, especially during the global financial crisis (GFC) of 2008.

However, the FRBMA's implicit rationale of implementing austerity as per monetarism continued to guide policymakers who had been trying to reach the fiscal limit on a priority basis in their budgetary policies. As was to be expected, the monetary and fiscal restraint were responsible for austerity in the economy, with untoward consequences for long-term growth, distribution and development.[4]

We need to point out here the further consequences of the rules under the FRBMA, by which the fiscal deficit has to be met by funds borrowed from the market at the prevailing interest rate, thus generating an interest bill in the fiscal budgetary account as a liability. The primary account, arrived at by deducting interest payments from the fiscal account, then goes through a compulsive squeeze on capital expenditure and social sector spending, both having their respective unfavourable impacts on growth and distribution. This provides one more instance of the steady drift of policies away from the previous goal of achieving a developmental state, as under the new regime of liberalized markets. This occurs not only with the direct contraction of public expenditure resulting from a cut in fiscal deficits, but also with the rule to borrow in the market to meet budget deficits. The related increases in interest liabilities in fiscal budget on borrowings simply pre-empts public investment and social sector expenditure, both part of the primary budget.[5]

As for India's GDP growth, a peak rate at 8.49 per cent was attained at the end of a decade after 1991, in 2010, preceded by a volatile trajectory. It was followed by distinct downward slides in the growth rate, especially with the impact of geopolitical and Covid-19 pandemic shocks over the next few years. It must be noted, however, that with the implementatation of policies that gave rise to austerity and increased inequity, the GDP growth rate

FIGURE 4.1 *Gross domestic product of India, constant prices* per cent changes

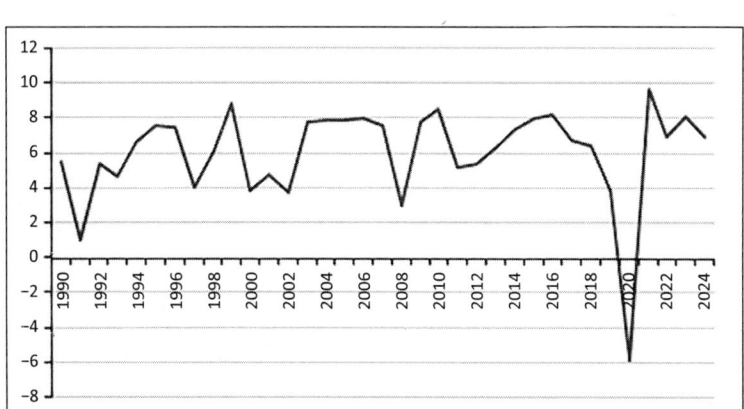

Source: International Monetary Fund (IMF), *World Economic Outlook Database*, October 2024.

even at its peak was incapable of generating development in the domestic economy.[6]

Policies devised in India to attempt inflation-targeting closely followed the recommendations of two official committee reports on monetary reforms, submitted by Narasimham, a former governor of the country's central bank, the RBI, in 1991 and 1998.[7] The reports advocated use of the mainstream dictum of austerity as a tool for controlling inflation. Their recommendations, as implemented, brought about the above-mentioned change in the prevailing system of deficit-financing. In line with the recommendations of the committee reports, it became obligatory for the government to meet fiscal deficits with funds raised in the market by selling government bonds, rather than by borrowing from the RBI. The step, which was consistent with mainstream principles as a useful tool to curtail the inflationary impact of deficit finance, was also responsible, as already mentioned, for additional expenditure on the accrued interest charges in the fiscal budget which resulted from sales of bonds. In effect, this remained responsible for curtailing the sum which could be allocated in the primary budget to meet expenditure on public investment and the social sector.

End to Financial Inclusion

With economic policies drifting away from a development-oriented approach, there was a reallocation of the 40 per cent (priority) bank credit directed to borrowers who were not always from the category of the poor. In addition, permission was given to banks to charge interest rates freely on loans above Rs 0.2 million, removing the cap which had so far prevailed on such small loans given essentially to smaller industrial concerns or poor individuals.

Further, the distribution of the priority credit, while remaining at 40 per cent of bank deposits, became grossly unequal.[8] In agriculture, which continues to provide a livelihood to nearly

70 per cent of India's population, the share of priority credit has been only 18 per cent. And even out of this small share, marginal farmers (with landholdings not more than 1 to 2 hectares) could avail loans of only up to Rs 0.2 million. This stands in stark contrast to the Rs 500 million which was set as the upper limit of credit to enterprises in the category of micro, small and medium enterprises (MSMEs), which too was given a share of 7.5 per cent in priority credit. A similar dichotomy prevailed in the provision of priority sector loans of up to Rs 3.5 million, to help low-cost housing in metropolitan areas. Finally, concern about possible defaults continued to guide an inclination to screen the credit-worthiness of each loan, in line with the insistence of the banking lobby which is in close alliance with the state.

Financial reforms in the country also acted as a major incentive to change and minimize the functioning of the existing development banks, which so far had been offering long-term credit at concessional terms to finance developmental projects. The development banks were turned into regular profit-making commercial banks, dealing a heavy blow to the banking sector as a source of developmental credit. Simultaneously, the responsibilities that the RBI so far held in relation to the development banks also came to an end. Thus, the changing scenario signified an *end to the inclusivity of finance in India's banking sector, all in the name of an 'efficient' banking industry as advocated under neoliberalism.*

Financial inclusion in India was subjected to further setbacks when capital adequacy ratios (CARs) were instituted by the Bank of International Settlements (BIS) in 1988. The screws were tightened further by introducing risk calculation ratios in terms of the CRAR (capital-to-risk weighted assets ratio), the capital adequacy ratios under Basel III.[9] As mandated by the CRAR, banks in India were required to maintain equities at 9 per cent of risk-weighted assets in their portfolios. The successive increases in the CARs since their inception in 1988 has retarded financial inclusion, especially by instituting itemized tier-wise risk assessment as already provided in the Basel II norm. The differentiated risks on loans to different categories of clients made it extremely difficult for the poor and the marginalized to get credit from banks. Most of them had little to put up as collateral, and so found it difficult to access credit.[10]

Rising Pace of Financial Liberalization: The Impact

Two other major changes further faciliated and increased the pace of financial liberalization: the entry of foreign institutional investors (FIIs) to the Indian stock market in 1992,[11] and convertibility of the current account in 1993. We will draw attention later to the related spurt in financial activities, especially in the rising capitalization of India's stock markets, most of which came as a result of the above sanctions.

Alignment with neoliberal policies and inflation-targeting were further reinforced in India with the recommendations of the Chakravarty Committee (1985). Capital account convertibility (CAC) was recommended a decade later by a committee headed

FIGURE 4.2 *India: central bank policy rate* per cent per annum

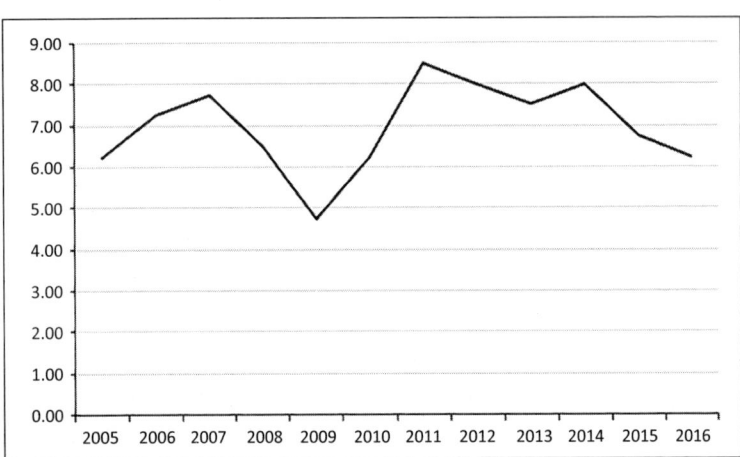

Source: International Monetary Fund (IMF), *International Financial Statistics*.

FIGURE 4.3 *India: lending rate* per cent per annum

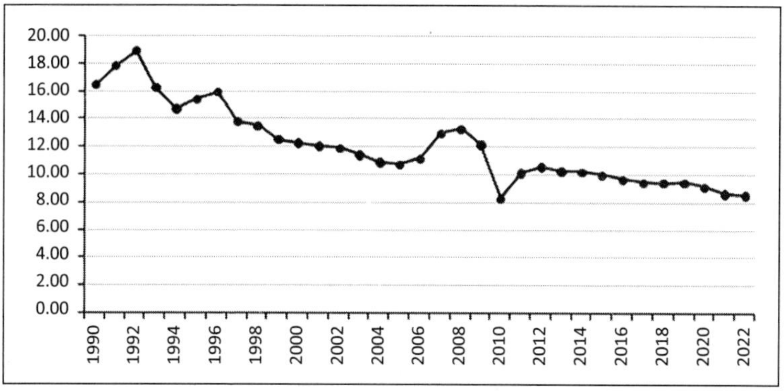

Source: International Monetary Fund (IMF), *International Financial Statistics*.

by S.S Tarapore (1996), but the proposal could not be implemented – largely due to the onset of the global financial crisis (GFC) within a few years, in 2007–08.[12]

Inflation-targeting had to deal with the management of *policy interest rates as a major tool*. The onset of GFC (2007–08) led to downward shifts in policy rates in most countries. India *did not* reduce the policy bank rate after 2008, while the lending rate, already on an uptrend since 2005, went further up after 2010, and then on a steady downward incline over the next few years. This followed the changing interest rate policy of the US Fed, marking the first phase of quantitative expansion (QE1) during which the reduced Fed rates reached the lower bound around zero.[13]

In 2010, when the Fed announced a second round of quantitative easing, the Fed rate was still at its lower bound. As in the EMEs of Latin America, India continued to pitch high its policy rate (bank rate of interest) (Figure 4.2). This was to contain or target inflation that could result from the rise in capital inflows from the US as a consequence of the US Fed rate approaching zero, and also to attract capital flows. The high policy rate in India also continued when the rates in the US were pushed up to control domestic inflation in the US after 2013, described as post-QE taper tantrum. Indian policymakers considered it important to continue with the incentives to capital flows from abroad by pitching the policy interest rate high. Apprehensions in India and in other developing countries of possible declines in the inflows of capital due to high rates in the US also worked to stiffen their respective domestic interest rates.

High policy interest rates continued in India, with periodical adjustments by the RBI to take care of the ongoing inflation. The response was a strategy to avoid capital flights from the country. On the whole monetarism, without fail, continued to guide the direction of policies through all these changes in India and in other EMEs.

Further Constraints in Fixing Domestic Interest Rates:
An Impossible Trilemma
It is relevant here to refer to the restraints that are *generally* faced by developing nations on fixing their policy rates (of interest), while continuing with liberal (free) capital flows and managed exchange rates. The problems, identified in the literature as an *impossible trilemma*,[14] arise as excess net inflows of capital enter the domestic market under deregulated finance and push up the nominal exchange rate of domestic currency in terms of foreign currencies (say, the US dollar). When there is exchange rate appreciation, attempts are usually made by the monetary authorities to adjust the rate at a desired level. This is done by sterilizing the excess inflows of foreign currency, by purchasing foreign currency with domestic currency. The foreign currency adds to the official reserves, which, being high-powered money, contributes to M2.

A rise in M2 prompts the monetary authorities to target inflation in the domestic economy, both through monetary tightening (high interest rates) as well as fiscal stringency, like the FRBMA in India as discussed above. The outcome leads to an *impossibility* on the part of host economies (which are usually in the developing regions of the world) to achieve all *three* targets – namely, autonomy in monetary policy, managing the exchange rate and freeing capital flows – simultaneously. Since the last two normally prevail in terms of their accepted policies, what gets left out is autonomy in the choice of a domestic rate of interest that is consistent with the needs of the economy. A stiff interest rate is obviously contractionary for such economies.

Attempts on the part of the government to manage the exchange rate and liberalized flows of capital thus put pressure on the monetary policy with interest rate no longer at an appropriate level – an outcome reflecting the 'impossible trilemma'. In addition, expected changes in the exchange rate of the domestic currency, which is non-convertible, are reflected at the forward exchange rate moving at a higher level in relation to the spot rate. To keep parity, the domestic interest rate needs to be fixed with a premium over the foreign rate, thus bringing in an added upward pressure on the domestic interest rate in the market.

The rate of interest in the domestic economy has a link to *interest rate parity*, subject to risk premium on the exchange rate of the domestic currency. Given the global currency hierarchy and the non-convertible status of developing country currencies, the risk premium on those is usually positive. Thus, $i_d - i_f = E^f - E^d$, where i_d and i_f represent domestic and foreign interest rates respectively, while E^f and E^d relate to forward and spot exchange rates of the domestic currency in terms of a unit of foreign currency. With a positive spread between the forward and spot exchange rates – which indicates a possible depreciation of the domestic currency in future – the domestic interest rate, to attract capital, usually has to be fixed at a level higher than the foreign rate.

Given the rating of currencies in the global currency market, which is determined by the convertibility status of individual currencies, the majority of developing countries (which include India) fix their interest rates at levels which are much higher than the foreign rates. The aim is to attract foreign capital by offering relatively higher interest rates in the domestic economy, along with appreciated exchange rates of their currency. Thus, there has been an additional pressure on domestic monetary authorities in developing countries including India to keep an upward margin in the domestic interest rate even beyond its parity to the foreign interest rate. This can be viewed as an indirect consequence for weak currency economies like India and many other developing countries subject to non-convertibility of their currencies in global currency markets and a low status in the global currency hierarchy.

Inflation-targeting in Practice in India
Of late, a monetary committee has been instituted by the RBI to decide on changes in policy bank rates of interest on a quarterly basis. To determine the rate, there is reliance on the index of prices as in the consumer price index (CPI). While this sets a direction to the expected changes in the interest rate, the fixing of the rate is also influenced by the expected changes in exchange rates of domestic currency.

Inflation-targeting under monetarism also has a role in the contraction of fiscal expenditure.[15] This was initiated in India with the implementation of the FRBMA of 2003, in terms of which, as mentioned above, the fiscal deficits of the treasury could no longer be financed by the RBI. Instead, they had to be financed with borrowings from the market, which entailed a proportionate interest liability to be met in the fiscal budget. With expenditure in the primary budget[16] related to defence being rather inflexible, the consequence has been a further squeeze on remaining expenditures in the primary budget, which include capital investments and social sector subsidies.

Changes as described above in India's monetary and fiscal policy point to an abandonment of earlier goals – to have autonomy in settling domestic economic policies and to have financial inclusion.

RBI GOVERNORS ON FINANCIAL LIBERALIZATION

It is interesting to look at the views expressed by different RBI governors on financial liberalization. Those have been individuals who can be recognized as major architects of the monetary reforms in the country.

We first consider Raghuram Rajan, an academic from Chicago University who served the International Monetary Fund (IMF) between 2003 and 2006, before his stint at the RBI during 2013–16. While expressing his firm faith in inflation-targeting and in the tools to achieve it as prescribed in previous committee reports,[17] Rajan recommended the use of CPI in place of wholesale price index (WPI) which, according to him, was less representative of price movements, especially for retail trading.[18] This was a much-needed and major change in policy.

As far as financial inclusion was concerned, Rajan held that 'we have tried in the past lending to priority sectors through mandates. … and what was archived was still … too far short of goals'. He believed that 'the market will take care of needs',[19] as illustrated by SEWA in Gujarat, and possibly also by using technology. He also wanted banks to be freed from government intervention, a position conforming to his view on 'mandated' priority loans.

There was a bit of a contrast between Rajan's views and those of Y.V. Reddy, who was governor of RBI during 2003–08. As he mentioned in an interview,[20] while referring to official policies with the twin goals of stability and financial inclusion, he thought that while a lot of attention was paid to stability, financial inclusion lost its way in terms of the implementation of policies. This was despite some limited institutional reforms like the Pradhan Mantri Jan-Dhan Yojana (PMJDY), but on a scale *not* commensurate to cover all. Reddy had a sarcastic comment to make on the emerging pattern of financial inclusion: '… are we trying to have two financial systems: those meant for the poor and those meant for the non-poor?'[21]

It is useful to note that financial inclusion was officially acknowledged in India as *access* to financial services, as distinct from credit *per se*. The distinction was drawn in a special official report (2008) on financial inclusion under Rangarajan, a former governor of RBI.[22] In this context, Reddy made the point that with technology now offering a digital breakthrough, financial inclusion is expected to be demand-led, for example with demands to open accounts to enable direct benefit transfers![23] However, with the coming up of the digital divide, many clients of banks are incapable of asserting or even communicating their demands to the appropriate authorities.

In general, the implementation of financial inclusion in India turned out to be difficult due to the clear absence of official prioritization in the face of the adoption of neoliberal policies over the last few decades.

INFLATION-TARGETING CONTINUES TO DETERMINE POLICY RATES IN INDIA IN THE FACE OF QE-RELATED CHANGES IN US FED INTEREST RATES

The use of monetarist principles in inflation-targeting has continued over the years in India. The strategy can be observed in the high interest rate policy followed by the RBI, both during the QE between November 2008 and May 2013, and in the post-QE years till the current period (Figure 4.2).

While data for the policy rate have not been published by the RBI beyond 2016, the lending rate set by the RBI rose to 10 per cent and more in 2015, followed by a marginal declines in the following years and peaking above 10 per cent by 2023 (Figure 4.3).[24]

As for inflation-targeting in more recent years, from 2016, the interest rate in India has been set by the 'monetary committee' set up by the RBI to fix the rate by adjusting with the rate of inflation as recorded by the CPI index. Even during the pandemic years of 2020–23 the high levels of interest rates in India were set according

FIGURE 4.4 *US Fed interest rates*

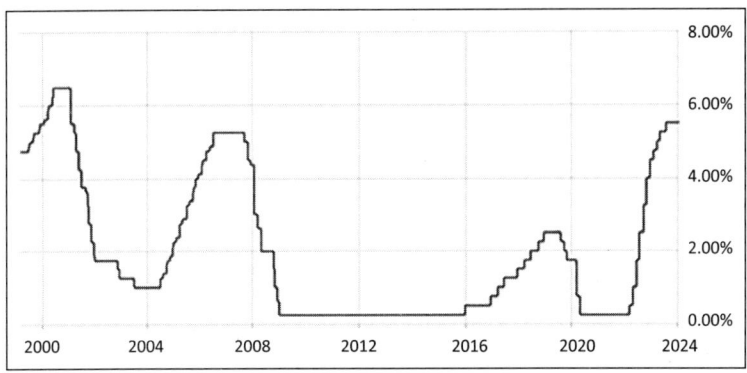

Source: https://tradingeconomics.com/united-states/interest-rate.

to the pace of domestic inflation. It can thus be observed that the flattening of Fed interest rates in the US to near-zero during 2008–16, and more recently between March 2020 and November 2023 (Figure 4.4), had no impact on India to emulate by adjusting the high policy rate to a lower level. Instead the *official goal of inflation control continued to stiffen interest rates*, more to avoid sudden flights of short-term capital away from the country.

Official Reserves Maintained in Excess on a Precautionary Basis
As mentioned in earlier chapters on Latin America, there have always been apprehensions that there could be a run on the country's stock of official foreign exchange reserves with an unforeseen crisis in the balance of payments. This often prompted the monetary authorities, in such situations, to hold their reserves at levels which were more than adequate under normal circumstances. As mentioned, the literature refers to such a situation – where reserves are held in excess on a precautionary basis – as reflecting a 'quadrilemma'.[25] With convertible currencies like the US dollar having the highest rating in the prevailing international currency hierarchy, most non-convertible currencies (like the Indian rupee) held by the developing countries are ranked

low in the hierarchical order of currencies. For these countries high levels of reserves held in convertible currencies are treated by their officials as prudent measures to take care of unforeseen attacks on their domestic currency and balance of payments.

Maintaining large reserves to meet sudden flights of capital from the country, however, turn out to be costly for these domestic economies. This is because the interest earned on those reserves are either nominal or relatively low (as for example on US Treasury bonds) as compared to market rates, which entails losses for the country concerned.

Official reserves in India rose to a peak of nearly $540.72 billion in 2020–21 before tapering off over the next couple of years and reaching $506.91 billion in 2022–23, largely due to the pandemic-led global recession. In this, a steep upward climb in reserves, from nearly $241.42 billion in the post-GFC years of 2008–09 to the current peak, is noticeable (Figure 4.5). The urge to maintain excess reserves on a precautionary basis obviously reflects the weak status of the rupee in the international currency hierarchy. Paradoxically, this is made possible with the inflight of

FIGURE 4.5 *Official foreign exchange reserves of India*

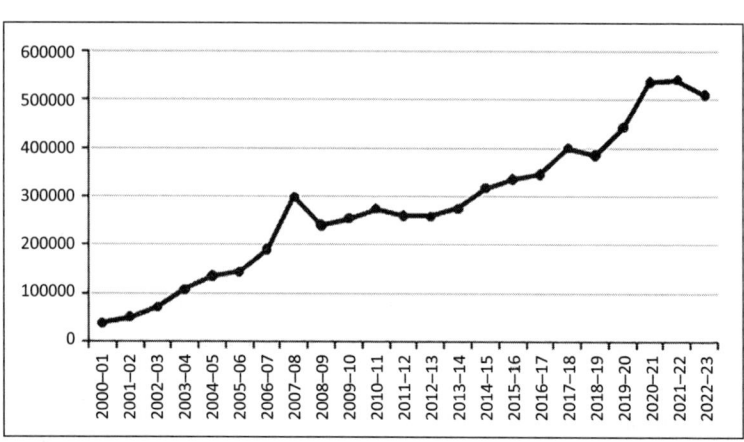

Source: Reserve Bank of India (RBI), *Handbook of Statistics on Indian Economy*.

short-term capital which makes possible the rising reserves.

The exposure of the rising official reserves to short-term capital inflows exposes the country to sudden withdrawals, which, *ironically,* makes it important to hold reserves in excess as compared to a level that could be considered normal for the country.

Financial Liberalization and the Rise of the Financial Sector: Quantitative Weight and Qualitative Support

In India, net inflows of both direct and portfolio capital have been subject to considerable volatility over the last two decades. Of the two, net portfolio flows, as expected, display a greater degree of fluctuations while net FDI, subject to some volatility, also showed a rising trend.

The rising pace of short-term capital inflows to the country can be linked to the growing capitalization of India's stock markets, given that it still remains the major destination of short-term flows. Thus, the Sensex or the Bombay stock price index, with

FIGURE 4.6 *Net flows of FDI and portfolio capital to India*

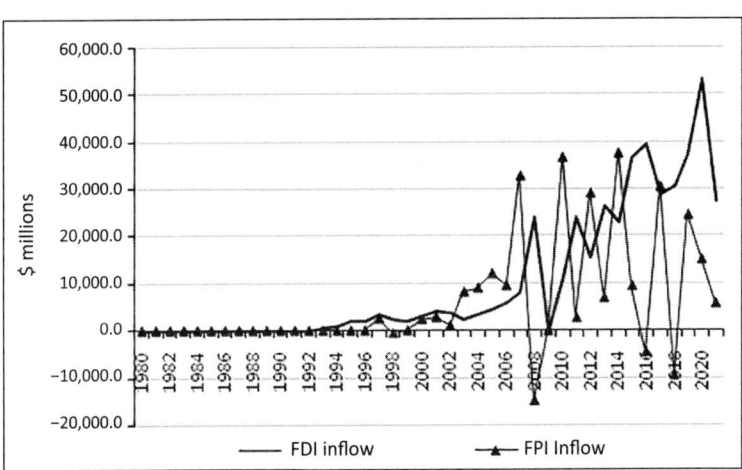

Source: International Monetary Fund (IMF), *International Financial Statistics*.

FIGURE 4.7 *Stock market capitalization* Rs crores

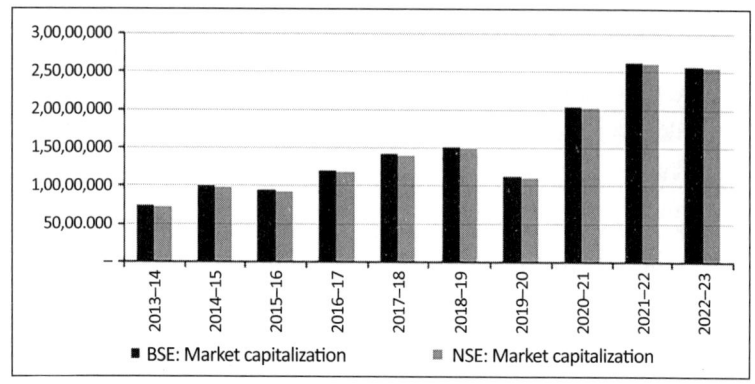

Note: Rs 1 crore = Rs 10 million.
Source: Bombay Stock Exchange (BSE) and National Stock Exchange (NSE) as cited by SEBI, https://www.sebi.gov.in/reports-and-statistics/publications/jul-2020/handbook-of-statistics-2019_44233.html

base in 1978–79, rose more than twenty times between 1991–92 and 2020–21. This was reflected in rising market capitalization, which multiplied by more than five times between 1990–91 and 2020.[26] These changes were accompanied by rising volatility and an uptrend in both portfolio flows and stock prices.

Deregulation in India's capital market permitted, among others, access of FIIs to the country's stock markets, foreign exchange markets and, lately, commodity markets. This generated frequent bubbles in the markets, largely due to the entry of volatile and short-term FII flows. As was to be expected, stock market turnovers were matched by similar changes in net inflows (liabilities) relating to derivative instruments – which also indicated an increase in the investments of short-term capital inflows as derivatives. None of this, however, had any bearing whatsoever to real transactions.[27]

Financialization, signalling the related changes in India's financial sector, also influenced the pattern of investments by non-financial corporates in the country.[28] In India, as it happened elsewhere, higher returns on financial assets (as compared to the average returns in industry) affected the composition of portfolios held by non-financial corporates. The data available indicate that there has been a steady rise in the share of financial assets in portfolios held by non-financial corporates.[29]

Evidently, changes as above suggest a pattern where investment in the real economy was of a lower priority even for the non-financial corporates in India's private sector. Of late, the data on household savings indicates a similar pattern, with financial assets having a major share in the portfolio of household, as can be explained by the ongoing wave of financialization.[30]

Finance Rose to Dominance amid the Structural Changes in the Indian economy

Structural changes in the Indian economy over the last few decades provide further explanations of the relative expansion of the financial sector which took place along with a rapid rise of finance-related services. The structural changes can be seen in the differing contribution of different sectors to aggregate output (GDP) over this period. The share of the services sector in GDP has continued to be well above that of industry since the mid-1990s. In addition, its share in absolute terms has been on a steady rise over time. Of items within the services sector, finance contributes the maximum, both in terms of rapid turnovers and *high-value* financial transactions. It is thus but natural that the rising share of the services sector in the GDP is accompanied by a similar rise in the share of finance-related activities in GDP.

Agriculture contributes a low share to the GDP in India, but the sector continues to provide livelihoods to large numbers of people engaged in activities in rural areas – which explains the low average income earned by those employed in the agriculture sector, in formal or informal capacity.

The share of industry in GDP, which has consistently performed with low and declining rates of growth over the last few decades, has also been low. The large and growing number of informal jobs available within the industrial sector have often been at remuneration levels which are lower than subsistence wages. The pattern is the same for the large number of people employed in the informal sector, *both* in agriculture and in industry, providing livelihoods for the majority of the population, which are at a precarious level.

The rising share of the services sector in India's GDP, especially witnessed since the mid-1990s, has within it a rise in the share of the financial sector, which includes the predominant 'financial, real estate and professional services' (or finance, real estate and business services, FINREBs), mentioned in earlier chapters.[31]

The pattern in recent years can be observed in Figure 4.8, which shows the share of services in the GDP at 63 per cent in 2022–23. As calculated, of aggregate services, more than one-third (36 per cent) was contributed by items in the category of FINREBs.[32]

To repeat, with structural changes in the Indian economy which came with a rising share of the services sector alongside declining

FIGURE 4.8 *Sector-wise shares of aggregate output, base 2001–02* Rs crores

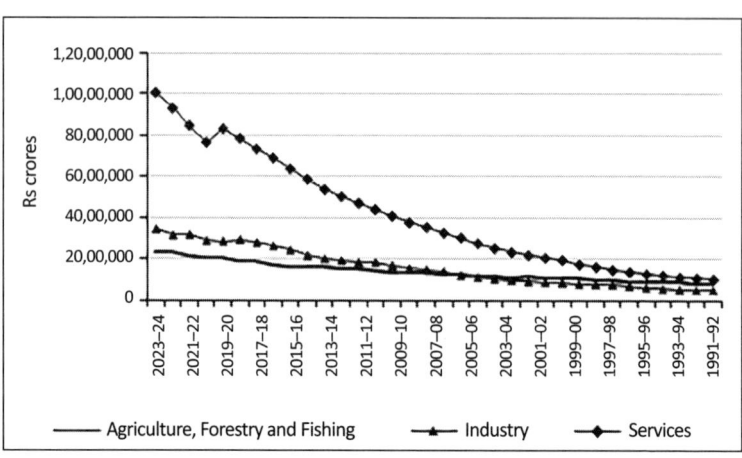

Note: 1 crore = 0.01 billion.
Source: Reserve Bank of India (RBI), *Database on Indian Economy*, and author's own calculations.

FIGURE 4.9 *Composition of services sector*

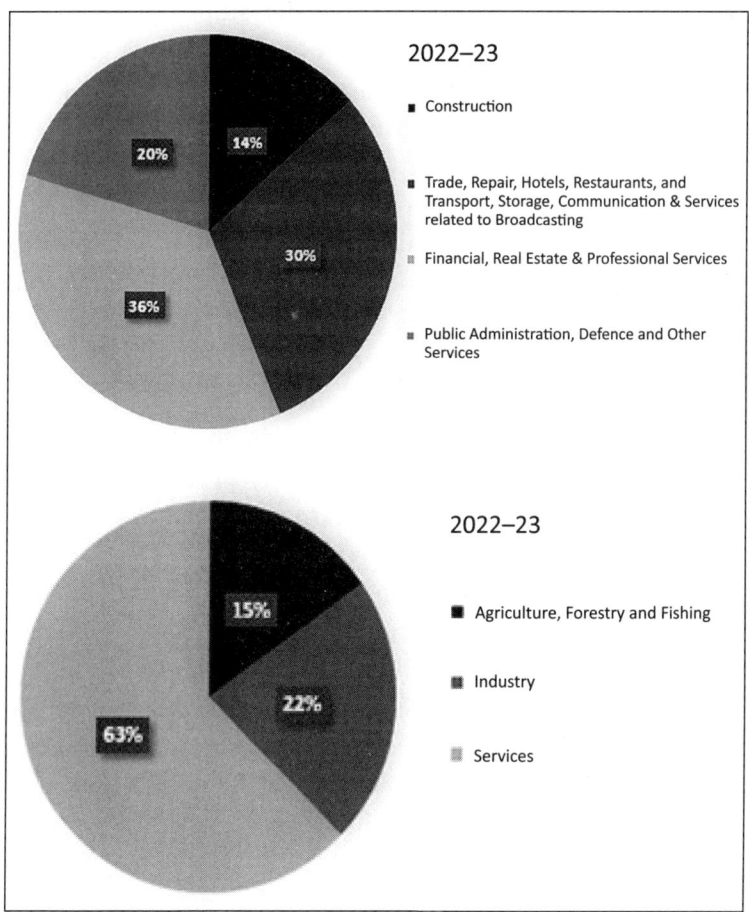

Source: As for Figure 4.8.

contributions of industry and agriculture, a major portion of the services sector consisted of finance-related activities. Unlike in the US or other advanced economies, the contribution of the services sector as a whole to employment has been rather low in India.[33]

As is the case in the EMEs of Latin America, the changing sector-wise shares in India's GDP along with the growing importance of the financial sector have a link to ongoing socioeconomic and political changes in the economy. Much of this is related to the facilitation and the state's open patronage of finance in these countries. These have been responsible for rapid expansion both of financial activities and the use of financial assets within the country. We will provide a more detailed analysis of the influence of socio-political aspects on the economy in chapter 5.

There also took place, under financial reforms and through measures initiated by the Indian state to facilitate the financial market, major transformations in institutions like banks and stock markets. It remains a fact that the Indian state, within a few years after the major shift to liberalization in 1991, was in close alliance with big capital in the domestic as well as overseas economies. This is evident from the continuing tax concessions offered in annual budgets of the country on corporate taxes, dividends as well as capital gains earned on financial assets by stakeholders.

As elsewhere, deregulation of finance in India has been responsible for generating uncertainty and speculative trading. A major consequence has been the wide-ranging use of derivatives to hedge against risks in India's financial markets, which has spread to the trading of stocks, real estate and even commodities. Most of these activities are financed by volatile flows of short-term capital – the volume of which sometimes even exceeded the steadier inflows of foreign direct investments (FDI) (see Figure 4.6).

Impact of Structural Changes in the Indian Economy

Structural changes were accompanied by major changes in the pattern of capital flows, with several implications for the Indian economy. The primary effect was the use of short-term portfolio capital for speculative investment in derivatives as a tool to hedge against risks on financial assets. Instruments innovated for derivative trading provided new opportunities for speculation, especially for footloose FIIs who had been permitted to invest in India's secondary stock markets since 1992. That deregulation of the financial market lent considerable steam to secondary stock markets in India can be seen from the rising capitalization experienced by the stock market (Figure 4.7).

It however remains a fact that the turnover of assets in the financial market was hardly linked to real activities. This is well observed in the pattern of financial booms in most EMEs with the presence of continuing real stagnation.[34] The pattern has been the same in India with the rather small value of shares sold as initial primary offers (IPOs), as compared to the large turnover of stocks sold in the secondary market, especially during boom periods. It may be recalled that while issues in the primary share market generally finance expansions or the creation of industrial plants, turnovers in the secondary market relate to multiple transactions of the same shares which are originally sold in the primary market. Hence, such transactions can only generate gains or losses for those holding financial assets on resale of papers in the secondary market.

As for the growth of employment, one can observe sharp differences in the contribution of different sectors of the Indian economy. Agriculture remains the largest provider of aggregate employment, at 45 per cent during 2023–24. The contribution of the services sector to share in GDP, while exceeding 50 per cent in recent times, is in contrast to its much smaller contribution to aggregate employment, at 28.9 per cent, in the same years.[35] The small contribution of service-related activities to employment is combined with an even smaller contribution by FINREBS, where most transactions are related to short-term, speculation-linked transactions.

The deployment of short-term capital in speculative profit-bookings have generated a typical bubble economy in India with the major source of profitability resting in finance. In effect, deregulated finance led the way to financialization, rendering financial assets relatively attractive and acting as a prime mover to lead investors in the direction of financial assets.[36]

Incidentally, the disproportionately large contribution of agriculture in aggregate employment is explained by the major presence of the informal sector in India, which has been providing nearly two-thirds of informal jobs in the country. Remunerations from these jobs very often do not cover even the subsistence requirements of those employed.

Thus, structural changes in the Indian economy have been a major factor behind the widespread poverty in the country, with nearly 70 per cent of the people seeking survival on less than \$2 per day. Jobs in industry, particularly in the formal sector, have been unavailable or scanty, leaving a vast majority either unemployed or employed on a casual basis in occupations fetching income at below-subsistence levels.[37] This contrasts with the financial sector's meagre contribution to job creation in the economy.

NEOLIBERAL POLICY IMPLEMENTATION IN INDIA AND SUBORDINATION

In this part of the section on India, we put together a brief account of the multiple ways in which subordination has already impacted India's official policies.

To reiterate, subordination in economies comes with an absence of autonomy for the state to choose and decide on policies which best suit the domestic economy. In India, as in similarly subordinated countries elsewhere, this has been the experience of the economy since a considerable period of time. The major operating forces behind this include the indirect strictures from overseas, which are transmitted via the market, for implementing neoliberal norms by relying on financial liberalization. The impact on domestic policies includes over-riding concerns regarding inflation in the economy and the adoption of inflation-targeting as a remedial measure. The result, as in the EMEs discussed in the previous chapter, has been the implementing of policies with high interest rates and reduced fiscal deficits in the economy.

As for the impact of inflation-targeting on fiscal policy, the signing of the FRBMA in 1992 put an upper limit to fiscal deficit as a proportion of the GDP. *The target for reducing the deficit, initially at 3 per cent of the GDP in terms of the FRBMA*, has remained a major goal in framing the annual budget. As mentioned above, unlike in previous years when the deficit could be met with funds provided by the RBI, it needs now to be market-financed by borrowing at prevailing interest rates. The interest bill, met in the fiscal budget, leaves less as expenditure in the primary budget.[38] Items which are affected in the primary budget include capital expenditure and social sector expenses including health and education. Defence, the remaining item of expenditure, cannot be cut for strategic reasons.

The implications of the above can be seen in the current budget estimates for 2025–26[39] (at the time of writing this book), which schedules the fiscal deficit at 4.4 per cent of GDP as compared to 4.8 per cent in the previous fiscal year. While the fiscal deficit as per the FRBMA is met by market borrowings, the interest liability at 25 per cent of budgetary expenditure has reduced the expenses on capital expenditure (15.5 per cent) as well as on the social sector (6 per cent) as proportions of aggregate budgetary expenditure. The impact reflects itself in the reduction of the primary budget deficit as a percentage of the GDP, amounting to only 0.8 per cent for 2025–26. This does not compare favourably with the higher fiscal deficit of 4.8 per cent for 2024–25. *Thus, fiscal discipline has been at the cost of growth-inducing capital expenditure and social sector expenditure for welfare as well as financial inclusion.*

Incidentally, as per the 'efficient market' principle of neoliberal theory, a free market by assumption dictates a minimal role for the government, which is considered to distort the functioning of the market. Ruling governments in the developing countries have been following such dictums by cutting back public spending and privatizing industry. Policy-making in India has followed all the above.

The fiscal restraints go hand-in-hand with similar restraints on monetary policy, which has been used as a tool to implement inflation-targeting in India. As observed, the interest rate has often been pitched high to contain the pace of inflation with periodic adjustments by the monetary committee of the RBI, as mentioned above. The outcome has often been a further tightening of the monetary policy. The bank rate, adjusted by the RBI according to changes in prices, basically has been using the principle of inflation-targeting. It is worth mentioning here again that interest rates continued to be high in India *both* during the QE and the reversal of QE in the US,[40] for reasons which include concerns about inflation as well as to attract capital flows from abroad.

The bank rate in India rose to an unprecedented peak of 8.10 per cent in 2011, having substantial recessionary consequences. The steep climb in the rate which continued up to 2015, however, was the RBI's response to the rising CPI index at home, and also to provide better returns for capital inflows in the face of stiffening of Fed rates in the US.

High interest rates were also meant to provide a favourable deal for those holding deposits in the domestic economy. Those with financial assets stood to gain by carry trade, using borrowed funds from abroad at relatively lower interest rates and investing the same at higher interest rates in the domestic economy. Finally, a hike in the domestic interest rate, in principle, was considered to encourage (as well as to retain) capital flows from abroad, offering enhanced earnings to overseas lenders on investments in domestic currency.

Repeating the other three hurdles to autonomy in India's monetary policy, those included the trap of an *impossible trilemma*, with difficulties in choosing the interest rate at a level that suits the country. In addition, there was the issue of *interest rate parity*, with wider margins between domestic and foreign interest rates to cover the high risk on the exchange rate of the domestic currency, subject to non-convertibility and having a low status in the global currency hierarchy. It called for a risk premium by putting upward pressure on the domestic interest rate to cover the risk. *Autonomy to control the domestic interest rate in all these cases was thus denied to the capital-importing developing countries.*

Policies of subordination also include, in India, the need to set official reserves at levels often above the normal level. This is because, by the logic of subordination, optimum levels of official reserves cannot be availed by such countries. Instead, the country maintains an excess level of the stock with a precautionary motive.

It remains for us to point to the third constraint, the movements in the exchange rates of the Indian currency. The adjustments of exchange rates in India have had a different course as compared to that in Brazil or Argentina where frequent changes in currency regimes (the Real Plan and the Austral Plan) were responsible for overvaluation of their currencies, much in accordance with the preference of the financial lobby. In India, attempts were made

FIGURE 4.10 *NEER and REER of rupee (40 currency basket), base 2015–16*

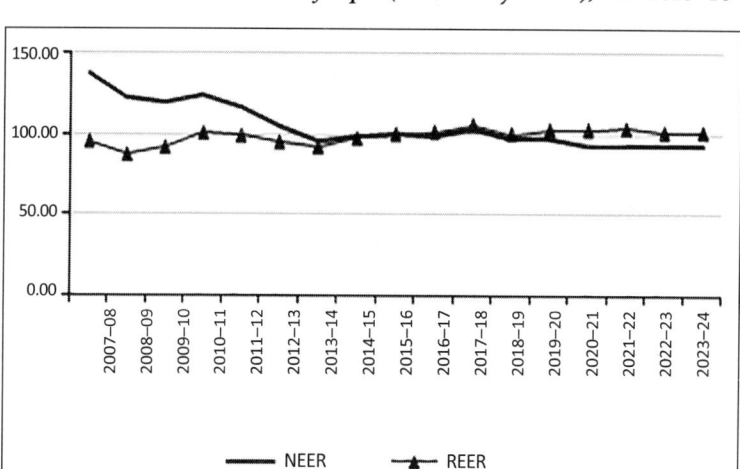

Source: Reserve Bank of India (RBI), *Handbook of Statistics on Indian Economy.*

by the RBI to control appreciation of the domestic currency by purchasing the inflows of foreign currency, which was largely to avoid loss of trade-competitiveness. While the forty currency-based nominal effective exchange rate (NEER) index of India displayed a downward trend from around 2010, the corresponding real effective exchange rate (REER) index was higher than the nominal index from around 2019 – with domestic prices rising more than the forty countries' weighted overseas prices, probably due to the pandemic and related price rise in the economy. *In effect, inflation-targeting did not work much to maintain the competitiveness of Indian products.*

The subordinate status of countries like India and other EMEs has also been actively fostered by *structural changes* that have taken place in their respective economies. These include the rising share of the services sector (in GDP), combined with its booming content of financial services and assets. As we explained earlier, this has gone with financialization of the economy with finance achieving domination and power over the economy.

There is an acknowledgement of financialization and the dominance of finance even in a current official report of the Indian government,[41] which mentions the impact of this on policy and resulting macroeconomic outcomes. Hopefully, policymakers will pay heed to such warnings.

The subordination of countries to neoliberal dictums on policymaking also relates to the alliance that prevails between the state and high finance in advanced economies. Unlike the era of the golden age of capitalism there, which lasted till the early 1970s (with overseas development assistance providing a bridge between the developmental states and the west under the tutelage of 'dependency'), the market today, allied to overseas governments, has taken over the agency of extracting surpluses from the same set of countries by using the neoliberal frame of economic policies.

ON SUMMING UP

Connecting the above threads, it is not difficult to identify a strong undercurrent as subordination that is in control of official policies in the EMEs including India. The restraints faced by India include a compulsive deregulation of the financial sector, largely in conformity with the mainstream advocacy of market efficiency. The impact includes the rising inflows of overseas capital to the domestic market and an immediate appreciation of the Indian rupee. The possible negative effects of an appreciated real exchange rate on trade balance led policymakers to act by buying foreign currency with local currency. This led to a rise in the official reserves, which is high-powered money, and caused expansion in M2. Official moves then targeted inflation by using fiscal-monetary devices and causing austerity in the economy. Subordination of the economy prevailed with the lost autonomy of domestic governments in fixing the interest rate or fiscal expenditure.

Hikes in interest rates also were used as a tool to attract foreign capital, a much-needed strategy for currencies (like the Indian rupee) having a low rank in the hierarchy of international currencies. Risks related to the non-convertible status of the domestic currency led to high-risk margins in fixing the interest rate, as in terms of the principle of 'interest rate parity'. Other issues of subordination include the well-known trap of an *impossible trilemma* faced by countries including India.

Acceptance has been the norm for subordinated nations like India with currencies of non-convertible status, also for maintaining excess reserves as a precaution against unforeseen crisis in the domestic balance of payments, even with low returns on investments of those reserves if any.

Moreover, once the market was liberated from the earlier regulations and attained the capacity to exercise surveillance, there emerged its power to react by penalizing subordinated countries for deviations if any. Examples include the possible initiation of fresh controls by a government on capital flows which could lead short-term flows to move away from the country, followed by expected downslides in official reserves and exchange rates. Further retribution could swiftly follow from credit-rating agencies like Moodys and S&P Global, and it often did enforce similar punishments on India in recent times.

THE TURN IN THE GEOPOLITICAL SCENE AND THE IMPACT ON SUBORDINATED DEVELOPING COUNTRIES LIKE INDIA

It will not be proper to end the discussion in this section on India without reference to the evolving geopolitics at the time of writing this book. In addition to the war fronts in the Middle East covering Iran, Russia and Ukraine, the issue at the moment especially relates to the newly elected US President Donald Trump's call for a trade war by exercising the hegemony and power enjoyed by that country, much of which is owed to the supremacy of the US dollar, the large US market and its defence capabilities over the years. The threat of a tariff-led trade war brings further uncertainty all over the global economy to which India will be no exception, especially with penalty rates of tariff at 50 per cent (which may be passé).

According to announcements made by Trump in early 2025, he will follow 'reciprocity' to fix tariffs on imports, which will be on an individual basis from respective countries. With tariff rates maintained by India in 2023 on an average 17 per cent higher than rates imposed in other nations including China, Trump claimed, at some stage, that he will retaliate by escalating tariff rates on imports from India to at least 17 per cent.[42] The current position, however, is more serious with a penalty rate of 50 per cent at the moment.

As for product-specific tariff rates in India, agriculture has received a much higher level of protection there with an average rate of more than 38 per cent in most years except the pandemic year of 2020. This rate has been much higher than that on non-agricultural items, which had a tariff rate of around 13 per cent in recent years. There is thus a strong likelihood that Trump will try to raise the tariffs on farm products imported from India, which has actually happened. So far the Indian government has held its position to protect the farming community by protecting the competitiveness of agricultural products.

This relates to the current 50 per cent rate of tariff on India's exports to the US – as penalty for being in the BRICS and for trading with Russia. On the whole, the situation projects rather dire consequences for countries like India and even Brazil with similar rates. It demands an overhaul of the current geopolitical order, not only on ethical grounds but also for global good and welfare. It is indeed difficult to predict the future turns of such matters, given the frequent turns in Trump-economics!

The current geopolitical conundrum will considerably add to the uncertainty already existing in India – pointing us somewhat in the direction of Keynes' famous statement on uncertainty, that 'about those matters we simply do not know' (Keynes 1937).

Deglobalization under a protectionist regime, especially in advanced economies including the EU, may also emerge with the onset of the trade war. For the developing countries outside that circle of rich nations, the hegemonic regime led by finance is likely to be matched by an authoritative trade regime which in all probability will further intensify the prevailing pace of stagnation in their real economy. In this scenario, India and other EMEs including the developing countries will be subject to tremendous disruptions in their domestic economies.

The 'invisible hand' of the market thus continues to follow the well-trodden track laid by neoliberal economics exercising its surveillance over subordinated economies like India.

COUNTRY PERSPECTIVES: CHINA

We now consider China, the other EME of Asia, which also went through deregulation of finance in the early 1990s. As in India, deregulation of the financial sector in China was launched at the end of an earlier regime marked by regulated and supervised finance.

Looking back, China has gone through three distinct phases of economic policies since the first phase from 1978, the year when its economy started getting integrated globally under Deng Shao Ping. This, however, was matched by a closely monitored strategy of what we describe as 'guided finance'.

The second phase started in 2005 with an end to the fixed exchange rate of the RMB and the initiation of several steps leading to further deregulation of the financial market, which led to instability. There took place a major turn in economic policies by 2020, under Xi Jinping. This marked a distinct third phase with an attempt to maintain autonomy in economic policies by following a 'dual circulation policy'. This final phase, marking defiance on the part of the country, is still continuing at present.

EARLY YEARS OF REGULATION IN CHINA UNDER 'GUIDED FINANCE'

Economic policies in China undertaken by Chairman Mao Zedong were subject to full autonomy with self-reliance till the year 1978, when Deng Shao Ping took over. The pattern started changing very slowly during the early years of Deng's regime with domestic economic policies gradually coming under the surveillance of external forces, especially with China joining the World Trade Organization (WTO) in 2003 and the opening up of markets which initiated the entry of foreign banks to the economy. However, one could identify in these changes a modified pace in official controls over capital flows, which has been described as 'easy in and difficult out'.[43]

During the Deng regime, the four state-owned banks of China – controlling 60 per cent of advances and deposits – were given a directive by the state council on *allocation of credit* with instructions to follow a 'guide book' set up for the purpose. Of the aggregate credit advances, agriculture got only 5.27 per cent, leaving the rest for industry; services at that time had a very small presence.[44] The device, providing a *direct link between banks, the state and industry*, generated a network that proved conducive to the economy whereby bank credit was channelized to stimulate industrial growth. Since bank credit was almost the sole source of finance in those days, it worked well for the economy.

Official controls over the financial sector, which we identified earlier as 'guided finance',[45] continued well with banks governed by 'segregated banking'. The four state-owned banks were responsible for advancing 80 per cent or more of aggregate credit flows to the economy during this phase. Funds also came from the overseas diaspora, mostly from Hong Kong, having close relations with Deng, which helped them to avail tax concessions. While credit from the state-owned banks was mostly distributed to state-owned enterprises, some of it was turned into non-performing, 'bad loans'. However, these were taken care of by the state.[46]

Stock markets, though less important than banks in providing credit, were under *strict regulation of the state* during this phase. Only one-third of shares, marked as 'B shares', were allowed to be traded in US dollar, and that too only by those officially identified as qualified foreign institutional investors (QFIIs). The rest of the shares, identified as 'A shares', were traded in RMB (renminbi). Many of these restrictions, as we point out later, changed with the 2005 reforms which permitted FIIs to hold 'A shares' in RMB subject to a lock-in period.[47]

China underwent global integration at a steady pace, which very soon secured for her a major position in the global economy.

FIGURE 4.11 *GDP growth rate of China, 1980–2023*

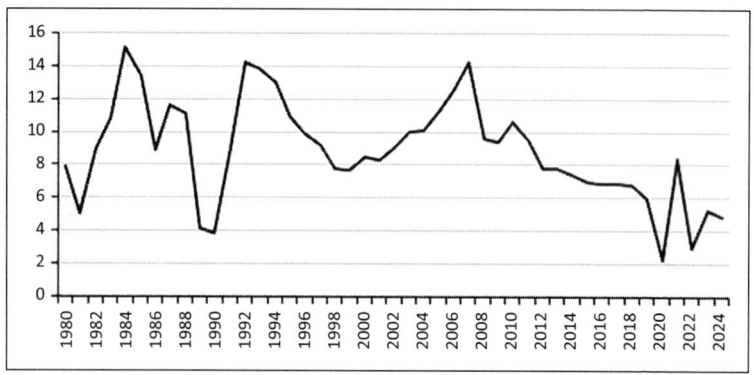

Source: International Monetary Fund (IMF), *World Economic Outlook Database*, October 2024.

There were unprecedented increases in the country's GDP growth between 1998 and 2007, matched by rising net exports, net inflows of FDI and rising exchange reserves. There was a twenty-fold rise in China's exports to Africa and Latin America between 1999 and 2019, and a near ten-fold rise in imports from the same countries over the same period.[48] In addition, a major share of China's exports reached the US market and the western world, thus completing China's global integration process.

The downtrend in China's GDP growth which started with the global financial crisis (GFC) in 2008 was to some extent managed through a stimulation package of $586 billion offered by the state.[49] Interestingly, China during the GFC performed much better than countries in the global North, especially the US and Western Europe, both of which suffered from severe recession.

The GDP growth rate of China in the post-Covid years faced sharp volatility due to the pandemic and geopolitical disruptions. These were responsible for an overall downward trend in GDP growth rate between 2010 and 2020, followed by 2022–23.

Deregulated Finance and Instability in China's Financial Markets: 2005 to 2020

End of Fixed ER with Floating of RMB in 2005: Temporary Appreciation of Currency

The system, however, was to go through a sea-change within a short time span at the end of the phase of regulated and guided finance. Reforms in China's financial sector took a distinct turn from the time Jiang Zemin took over from Deng Xiao Ping in 1993, continuing till 2003. His successor, Hu Jin Tao (2003–13) introduced a *major change* in the fixed exchange rate of RMB, which till June 2005 had been fixed at around 8.28 as period average per unit of US dollar. An announcement was made in July 2005 permitting the RMB to float in the market. As an immediate consequence, the exchange rate of the currency shot up by 2.2 per cent in the market, reaching RMB 8.07 per dollar on 21 July 2005. The rate per dollar appreciated much more over the next few years, touching 6.14 by 2014. By then Xi Jinping, the current president, was already in office.

With consumer prices in China moving parallel to those in the USA, which accounted for a major share of China's exports, the REER of the RMB moved parallel to the changes in bilateral nominal rates between the RMB and the USD. Starting from the 1990s, the upward movement of the REER touched the highest level in 2015. The REER of the RMB was also affected by a de-dollarization of transactions which linked the RMB to a four-currency trade-weighted basket consisting of the euro, yen, dollar and the Korean won. By this, the system replaced the previous dollar exchange rate regime.[50]

Ending US Allegations of 'Currency Manipulation'

It is well known that the floating of the currency which took place in 2005 and brought a noticeable appreciation of the nominal as well as REER rate of the RMB in terms of the US dollar, was a move long demanded by the US in the face of a fixed rate of the RMB over a long period. The matter had been subjected to repeated questioning by the US Department of the Treasury as one of 'currency manipulation'.[51]

Introduction of Universal Banking

Liberalization of overseas capital flows in China initiated with other financial reforms since 2005, contributed to the '... transformation from a mono-bank model to a multi-financial institutions system where five specialized state-owned banks ... were authorized to accept deposits and perform banking business'.[52] This initiated universal banking in China which led most of the capital inflows to reach the banks. Banks could now make more profits by doing business in the security market as permitted under the newly instituted universal banking of 2005.[53] This considerably enhanced the involvement of Chinese banks in security-related activities, as reflected in the Wealth Management Programmes (WMPs) which the banks offered to clients as part of their portfolio. The value of WMPs in 2019 was around $3 trillion, which, according to unofficial sources, was considerably large.[54] The use of WMPs also pointed to a rising pace of speculation in the market, as could be directly availed by bank customers.

Two-Way Floating of RMB: Further Currency Speculation

The floating of the RMB in 2005, which had led to currency speculation in China, was followed by another major change in the official currency management of the country. President Hu Jin Tao announced in September 2011 that the exchange rate of the RMB would henceforth be subject to *two-way floating*, covering both appreciation and depreciation.[55] In effect, this amounted to official endorsement that the RMB could henceforth depreciate.[56] Speculating on possible changes, there emerged a tendency in the market to short RMB and long dollar.

The change permitting the exchange rate to move in *either*

direction was viewed by some Chinese experts as an official signal to approve and encourage the use of the currency in international markets.[57] The central bank of China, the PBoC (People's Bank of China), published two reports in 2012 on this issue, with strong recommendations for capital account liberalization (CAL).[58] The suggestion was based on the post-GFC drop in asset prices abroad, which, as held, opened a 'window of opportunity' for Chinese investments abroad under CAL. It was also argued that the prevailing inefficiency in the management of controls in China by itself demands its closure.

The proposal, however, was critiqued by other scholars[59] who pointed at the implicit tautology in the argument of the PoBC on CAL initiating internationalization of the currency. They pointed out that capital controls remain the cornerstone of resource allocation in the economy, channelizing household savings to corporates and governments. Moreover, that the low rates of real interest currently earned by households in China on their savings in the domestic economy may lead to capital outflows under the CAL regime. Also, that the newly opened up arbitrage opportunities between the domestic and overseas rates of interest and exchange rates could further open up speculation under CAL.

The recommendations of the PoBC were not, however, implemented immediately. While the RMB continued to appreciate with the nominal exchange rate moving up (except for short interruptions) from 6.46 in 2011 to 6.14 in 2014, it underwent sharp depreciation in the next few years.

Widening Daily Trading Limit of RMB against Dollar Leads to Further Speculation: Depreciation of RMB after 2014

Currency management in China gave way to one more change in April 2012 when the daily trading limit of the RMB against the dollar was officially widened from 0.5 per cent to 1 per cent. With this widening of the daily trading limit of the currency by 50 per cent, further speculation surfaced in the market with expectations of possible depreciation of the currency. This actually took place in 2014 and the RMB continued to depreciate considerably, touching 6.95 per dollar by 2016. This was preceded by a currency crisis between 2013 and 2015.[60]

As mentioned above, the rising speculation was reflected in the changing portfolios of bank customers, having WMPs as part of their portfolio.

The earlier appreciation of the RMB as it rose initially after it was floated in 2005, met with some *downturns* in China's trade balance. It began with the global impact of the GFC between 2008 and 2011, and later between 2016 and 2018. An explanation can be provided for this decline in trade balance by the drop in net capital inflows during 2013–16, given that there was a close link between production in the FDI units and exports, with much of such output being regularly exported. One can here point to the related changes in foreign exchange reserves, which dropped from $4 trillion in 2014 to $3.10 trillion by 2023.[61]

Facts such as above, along with the declining flows of both FDI and portfolio capital between 2011 and 2016, generated some expectation in the market for depreciation of the RMB, which

FIGURE 4.12 *Balance of trade in China* in US dollars

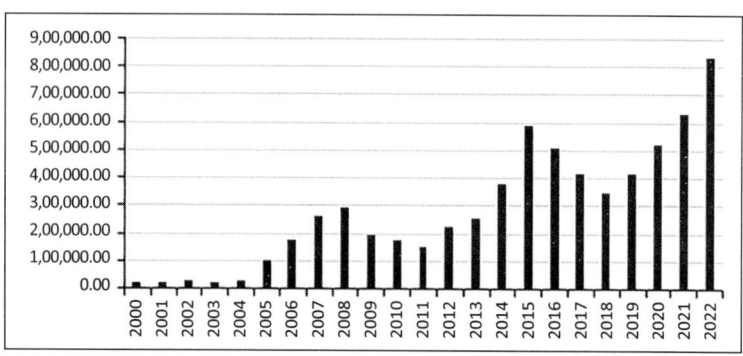

Source: International Monetary Fund (IMF), *International Financial Statistics*.

came about by 2015. This was favourable for the trade balance, generating surpluses between 2012 and 2015, and from 2019 onwards.

Turnaround in Capital Flows for China

Changes in the flows of capital to China include a substantial increase in the *net* inflows of FDI from 2005, shooting up to $2.31 trillion by 2011 – with the upturns largely responding to the floating of the currency which took place in 2005. Positive *net* inflows of FDI continued for some more time till 2013, and then again between 2016 and 2021, even after meeting the rising outflows directed to Latin America and Africa, the new foreign investment destinations of Chinese capital. The growing outflows, however, turned large enough to cause a $41.67 million *negative* net flow of FDI by 2016.

We draw attention here to the turnaround in the *net* FDI flows to China from around 2011. With sharp declines in the gross inflows of FDI and the rising outflows, net flows of FDI, as already mentioned, turned to near-zero in 2016 and were followed by sharp downturns in net negative flows during 2022 and 2023. This obviously marked a trend which was very different from that of earlier years with consistently large positive net FDI flows. As for portfolios, their net flows have often been negative since 2020.

The *declining net inflows* of FDI and portfolios in recent times stand out as a departure from what used to be normal in China. The change can be related to the ending of QE in 2013, when the Federal Reserve Bank of the US started raising interest rates to address domestic inflation. The new situation in the US was naturally expected to cast a shadow on capital flows to other countries in the South, and China was no exception. The adverse changes in the flow of gross FDI to China which came up were also affected, especially after 2020, by the Covid pandemic and geopolitical tensions in multiple locations of the world. However,

FIGURE 4.13 *Net inflows (liabilities) of FDI (foreign direct investment) and FPI (foreign portfolio investment)* in million dollars

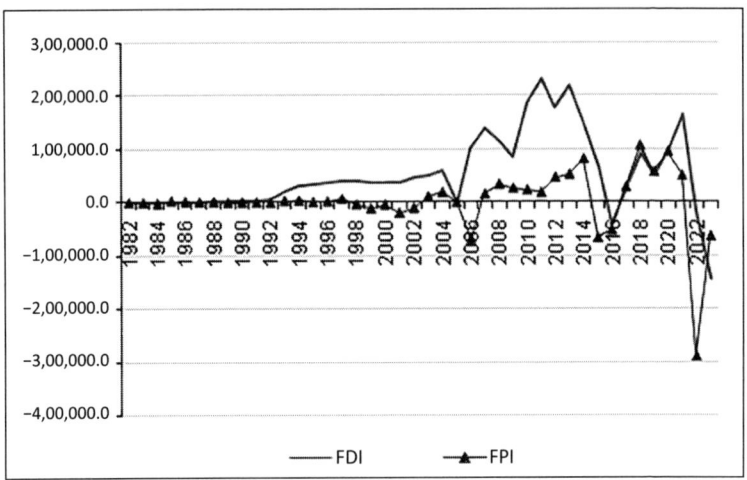

Source: Same as Figure 4.11.

FIGURE 4.14 *Gross inflows and outflows of FDI*

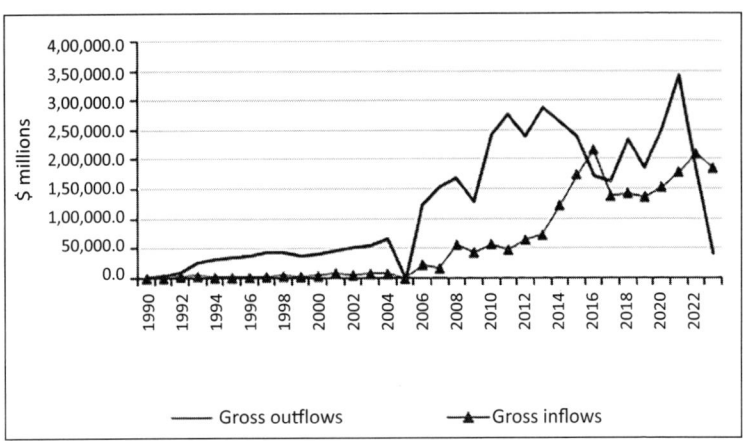

Source: Same as Figure 4.11.

notwithstanding such disruptions, net inflows of FDI to China rose by 2021.

Two important aspects relating to changes in capital flows as above need to be highlighted. First, about the gross inflows (liabilities) of FDI – with successive peaks between 2011 and 2021, each exceeding the previous one – there is a clear indication that there had been a *rise in flow of FDI in the direction of China during these years*. Second, the net negative sums of FDI that resulted in 2016 and 2022 were largely due to rising gross outflows (assets) as foreign investment from China.

The flow of net portfolio capital, as expected, has always been subject to sharp volatility in China. With its flow often turning negative, its footloose pattern was quite clear. Speculation related to the uncertainty of future RMB rates lent further steam to such volatility in the market. The rampant volatility of portfolio capital gained significance from 2005 onwards, when the fixed exchange rate of the RMB gave way to a floating rate. With further relaxation in the management of the exchange rate (as discussed above), the volatility increased further in the following years.

Net inflows of portfolios (with their related liabilities) were invested as derivatives in swelling volumes and with growing volatility, with temporary shortfalls.[62] Despite the official clampdown in China on the real estate market and on underground credit circulation, speculation continued unbridled in its economy. Much of the above resulted from successive changes in exchange rate management that had already taken place.[63]

Uncertainty in China's currency market, especially induced by changes in currency management, led corporates as well as traders in the market to hold on to the dollar, due to expectations of a depreciated RMB. In the meantime the country was subject to a currency crisis in between. In addition, speculation relating to the rate of exchange also generated some FDI outflows which in effect were in the form of capital flight from Chinese residents.[64]

Changes in the official economic policies also impacted China's

FIGURE 4.15 *Net inflows of FPI and derivative flows*

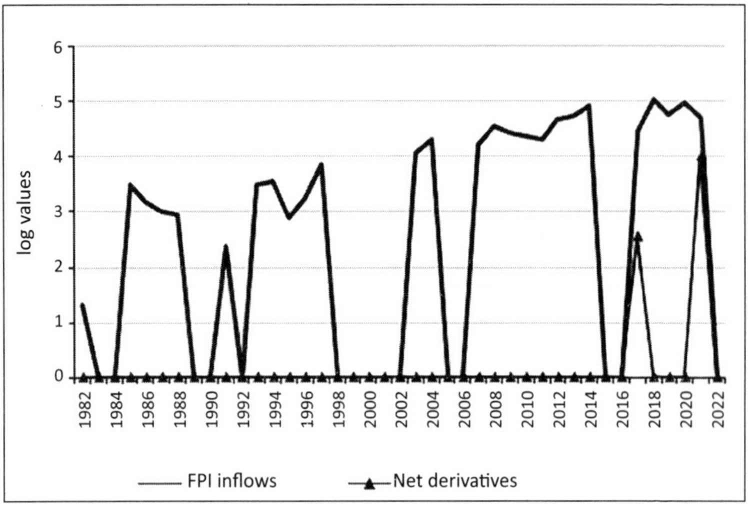

Source: International Monetary Fund (IMF), *International Financial Statistics*.

stock market, with finance from the stock market steadily rising from the previous 3.7 per cent of bank credit flows in 2013 to 12.42 per cent in 2017.[65] Growth in stock trading was further facilitated by official permission given to foreign investors to trade as the privileged category of 'Qualified FIIs'.[66] However, the easing of restrictions in China's stock markets which followed led to a sharp and unprecedented volatility in those markets after 2020, as indicated by the movements in the composite capitalization of the Shanghai stock market which rose from RMB 23.04 trillion in 2012 to RMB 91.61 trillion in 2023.[67] The earlier boom after 2012, however, was short-lived, and the Shanghai stock index dropped sharply with the crash of 2015 on 8 June, though it rose to newer heights thereafter. Volatility continued in China's stock market as a whole despite the continuation of the bifurcated stocks between tradeable (A) RMB shares and non-tradeable (B) dollar shares – as reflected in the hovering values of the composite index.[68]

Growing transactions as they took place in China's stock markets were visibly related to a similar growth in derivative transactions and net portfolio capital inflows, the latter providing the liquidity needed for transactions of the derivatives in the stock market. We notice in Figure 4.15, the close correspondence between the rate of changes in net FPI and net derivatives continuing from 2016, as plotted in terms of their respective log values.

STOCK MARKET CRASH IN 2015 LEADS TO EXCHANGE RATE VOLATILITY WITH DOWNWARD SLIDES

The rising uncertainty which led to a crash in the stock market in 2015 had a major impact on the Chinese economy. There were continuing fluctuations in the exchange rate of the RMB over the following years with a tendency towards depreciation. Further, the rising portfolio liabilities (inflows) subject to intermittent fluctuations with the entry of FIIs to the stock market, imparted further uncertainty. It may be mentioned again that the changes in currency management, considered in some circles as an attempt to attain international status for the RMB through convertibility, rather were responsible for imparting further instability in the market. The change in the situation was probably responsible for the sharp decline in China's official reserves from $3.8 trillion in February 2015 to $3.01 trillion in January 2017, followed by volatile flows and reaching $2.31 trillion by January 2025.[69]

Problems such as above were compounded by the revived US stricture on the exchange rate stability of the RMB, which was announced by President Trump as an ongoing deal in the trade war during his first presidential term, between January 2017 and January 2019. There was an implicit warning from the US administration at that time of open retaliation if the RMB was to depreciate in the future. An official announcement from the US cited that:

> ... China must also prepare for the possibility that the trade war will escalate into a currency war. If the renminbi comes under

devaluation pressure and the People's Bank of China does not intervene to stabilize its value against the US dollar, the US may label China as a currency manipulator.[70]

The above changes put China's policymakers in a quandary, with the global financial market facing the interest rate hikes by the Fed at the end of the QE in 2013 and China trying to stick to her goal of maintaining an expansionary policy through low domestic interest rates and a depreciating RMB. The problems were further aggravated with the outbreak of the Covid-19 pandemic, which affected China before other countries and quite severely; with the emergence of geopolitical tensions leading to war on multiple fronts; and finally, the return of Donald Trump in 2024 as president of the United States. Below, we discuss the new uncertainties that have been encountered by China since then, especially on the global trade front.

DEPRECIATING RMB AND XI JINPING'S DUAL CIRCULATION POLICY IN 2020: THE NEW PHASE OF ECONOMIC POLICY

The exchange rate of the RMB, as already mentioned, started depreciating very soon after its floating in 2005, with the decline recurring almost every alternate year from 2015 – and touching a low of RMB 7.25 to a dollar in February 2025.[71] Depreciations in recent times were also related to the pandemic (2020–21) and the Russia–Ukraine war, as well as the recently started Israel–Palestine war and attacks on Iran since 2022.

With the pandemic and geopolitics hitting the country hard while facing stagnating demand abroad, China launched a new strategy called 'dual circulation' in May 2020. Initially floated by the Polit Bureau of the Chinese Communist Party, the measure was endorsed by Xi Jinping.[72] This indicated a deviation away from the export-led growth model of 'international circulation' of Deng Xiao Ping to the 'dual circulation' policy of Xi Jinping.

The new strategy was to follow an *inward -looking economic policy, which focused attention on the domestic economy as a source of supply as well as demand.* China had been already following an expansionary strategy by keeping the interest rate low and a depreciated exchange rate. It became official with Xi Jinping's new policy of *dual circulation* in May 2020.

The exchange rate of China's currency depreciated successively in five out of seven years between 2015 and 2023. However, with the current rate of RMB at 7.25 to a dollar (as on 25 February 2025), which is relatively appreciated as compared to what prevailed as a fixed rate at 8.24 to a dollar over the decade preceding its floating in 2005, there can still be a turn on the part of the US administration with its *currency concerns.*

China Moves from 'International Circulation' (Export-led Growth) to 'Dual Circulation'

Depreciated exchange rates, low interest rates and expansionary fiscal expenditure indicated a significant turn in China's economic policy: from the model of 'international circulation' under Deng Xiao Ping to one of 'dual circulation' advocated by Xi Jinping. The strategy of 'dual circulation'[73] relied on a pattern of development that treats domestic circulation as the *mainstay,* while domestic and international circulation continue to reinforce each other. The purpose behind was to emphasize the importance of a positive reciprocity between domestic and international economic circulation. For China, it indicated an accelerated shift away from the previous export-oriented development strategy. Thus, China's exports, which stood at 35 per cent of GDP in 2007, had already come down to 20 per cent in 2022. In addition to the effects of the new policy on the domestic economy, geopolitics also had a role in pushing China towards the shift away from export-led growth – especially the pandemic of 2020, the ongoing war in Europe since then, and the Trump-led current trade war.

These developments led China under Xi Jinping to confirm the initiation of the 'dual circulation' strategy as above. It meant a 'rebalancing of China's economy away from a reliance on external demand as a stimulus to growth ("international circulation") towards increased self-dependence ("domestic circulation")'.[74] As already mentioned, it moved away from the export-led strategy of Deng Xiaoping, which had prevailed over the previous three decades.[75]

The tilt in policy in support of 'dual circulation' prompted China to continue with low interest rates along with successive depreciations of the RMB. These were steps much *in defiance* – not only of the inflation-targeting strategy adopted in the US in the post-QE years, but also of the follow-suit policies of the Latin American EMEs and India. All those countries still continue with their high interest rates and largely appreciated currencies, both as inflation rebuttal and as incentives to the flow of overseas capital.

Dual Circulation Strategy of China Continued During the QE Policy of the US Fed

The inward-looking strategy of China continued despite hikes in interest rates in the USA at the end of the QE, when Fed rates in the US were pushed up to control domestic inflation. China's lending rate of 6.56 per cent in 2011 continued to be reduced further to 4.35 per cent in 2015, and continued till 2023–24. The policy rate of the People's Bank of China (PBoC) fell even lower, to 1.90 per cent by 2023. Quite remarkably, the lending rate of the country was kept steady at 4.35 per cent all through 2015–23, which covers the post-QE years from 2013 to 2019 and the revived QE of 2020. Thus, China's domestic interest rates were not subject to changes because of external developments like the Fed rate adjustments during and after the QE. In contrast, external influences impacted domestic interest rates in other countries, including the EMEs we have discussed earlier.

Expansionary Monetary and
Exchange Rate Policies

As we can observe, there was *no noticeable adjustment of monetary policy* in China in response to changes in global interest rates including those in US federal rates. Nor was there any incentive to capital inflows provided in China by raising interest rates in response to declining net flows of FDI in the country.

It is important to highlight the fact that *the broad directions of China's monetary policy were never guided by the mainstream neoliberal theory of inflation-targeting*. Nor was it affected by changes in the US Fed rates of interest. Rather, China moved along a completely different trajectory, following a Keynesian expansionary path, which was suited to address the declining GDP growth in its economy since 2007–08.

China's policy to keep interest rates low and have a depreciated domestic currency which suited the expansionary goals set for the domestic economy was diametrically opposite to the strategy adopted by other EMEs in Asia or in Latin America, which was to respond to changes in exchange rates and in Fed rates in the US. As already pointed out in chapter 3 and in the section on India in the present chapter, those countries were pushing up domestic interest rates in order to control domestic inflation and, in addition, to arrest possible outflows of capital to advanced countries. Those countries also catered to an overvalued domestic currency to attract inflows of foreign capital. Both worked to deepen recession in the respective economies. China's responses to the same set of developments in the US were distinctly different.

On the whole, the exchange rate of the Chinese currency, at the end of its appreciation between 2005 and 2013 due to floating in the market, moved primarily in the direction of depreciation from around 2014. The change was related both to the new waves of speculation in the market on the currency rate as well as to the deterioration of China's trade balance during 2008–11. Much of

FIGURE 4.16 *Exchange rate of RMB to USD (average closing price)*

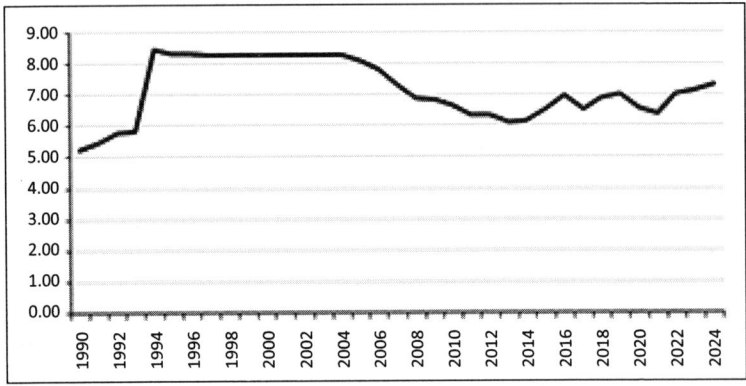

Source: https://www.macrotrends.net/2575/us-dollar-yuan-exchange-rate-historical-chart

FIGURE 4.17 *Real effective exchange rate (REER) of RMB, based on CPI*

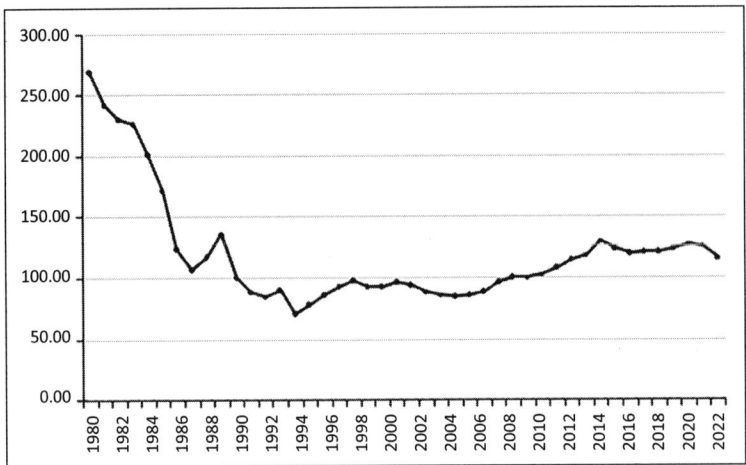

Source: Metadata by country, International Monetary Fund (IMF), *International Financial Statistics*.

the latter was in turn related to the reduced net flows of FDI over 2007–09, causing a loss of exportable goods produced by the FDI-controlled subsidiaries.

With the inbuilt vulnerability of export-led growth models based on 'international circulation' becoming visibly clear at the end of the global financial crisis of 2007–08,[76] and with the related recessions in the global economy, the shift to domestic circulation was viewed by China as an alternate strategy for reducing reliance on the rest of world. This was meant to avoid sudden shocks, both due to a sudden drop of supply or demand because of geopolitical and geo-economic factors, and due to a speculation-led collapse of financial flows in deregulated global markets.

China's turn in policy deviated from the pattern of responses of other EMEs, even to the tapering of the QE in the US. To repeat, the interest rate in those countries was pitched high, to curb possible expansion in domestic liquidity caused by the diverted inflows of short-term funds from the US. They continued with anti-inflationary measures despite having recession in their domestic economies. Looking back, we can view the continued use of low interest rates and depreciated exchange rates as a turn in China's economic policies.

The policy rate of interest did slide down in China, from 2.5 per cent in 2019 to 1.8 per cent in 2023. Since then it has stayed at around the same level till date, while policy rates elsewhere in other EMEs were rising. As mentioned above, low interest rate was one of the tools for the expansion of China's economy, along with other tools including a depreciating RMB exchange rate and fiscal support to the domestic economy.

There are quite a few factors behind the sharp turn in China's ongoing policies, including the property market crisis which was met with a government clampdown in 2021 on excessive borrowings by developers. As mentioned, the property market comprised '30% of the economy' or the GDP![77] The related problem has continued since then.

Another factor which worked to bring in the shift to 'inward circulation' was the downslides in China's trade balance – initially at the end of the GFC between 2009 and 2011, and later between 2015 and 2018. Given that the deterioration in trade could be related to the ongoing recession in the west, the drop in net FDIs, as well as to geopolitical developments including Trump's attempt in 2017 to initiate a trade war with China, moving 'inward' was probably considered by China as a better option, as officially announced by President Xi Jinping. The Covid pandemic which affected China and its trading partners could also be counted among the factors behind the move to the new policy of dual circulation.

Lastly, it has also been noted that China's reliance on microchips which are designed and fabricated overseas, and imported from the US and Europe, have been causes of concern in having a continuity of the country's recent policies.[78]

China's Monetary Policy and the Autonomous Path

There were external pressures on monetary policy in China, as in other nations in the global South, during the QE 1 to QE 3 phases of US Fed between 2008 to 2012,[79] and later during the post-QE years from 2013 to 2020, when the Fed was hiking domestic interest rates to tackle local inflation. In March 2020, a fresh round of QE 4 was initiated in response to the pandemic crisis, with a repeat of the low interest policy under QE (Figure 4.18).

Notably, China's expansionary fiscal-monetary policies have been continuing unabated in the post-QE years between 2013 and later years, with the lending rates of interest down from 6.56 per cent in 2012 to 4.38 per cent in 2015, a rate that has been continuing through the 2020s (Figure 4.20). The policy rate of the PoBC (the central bank) went through further downtrends – from 2.20 per cent in 2020 to 1.80 per cent by 2023 (Figure 4.19).

Use of the lending rate in China was combined with cash reserve ratios (CRRs) and sale/purchase of bonds, the other tools

FIGURE 4.18 *Fed interest rates during and after QE*

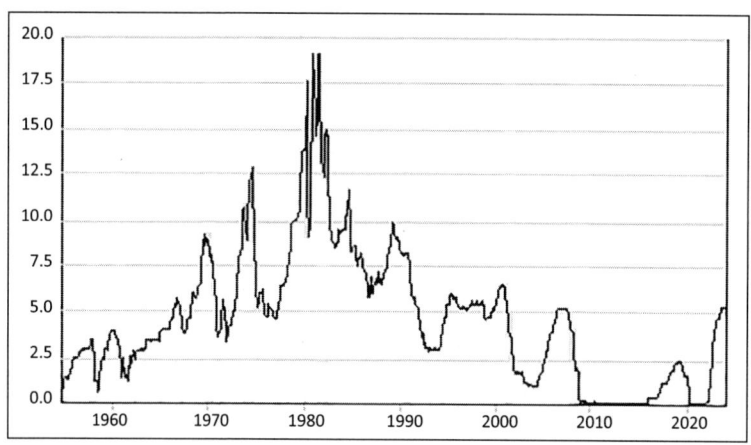

Source: *Federal Reserve Economic Data*, https://fred.stlouisfed.org/series/
FEDFUNDS

FIGURE 4.19 *Central bank policy rate, China,* per cent per annum

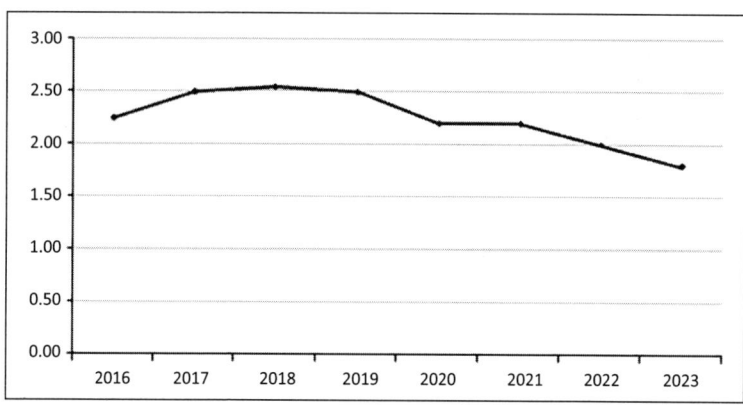

Source: International Monetary Fund (IMF), *International Financial Statistics.*

Figure 4.20 *Lending rates, China* per cent per annum

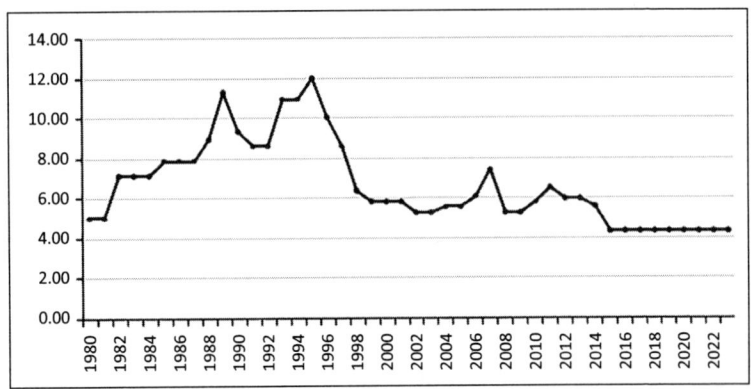

Source: International Monetary Fund (IMF), *International Financial Statistics.*

of monetary policy management. Data available from CEIC, the Global Data Indicator,[80] show successive decreases in China's CRR over the last ten years, from 21 per cent in 2012 to less than 10 per cent in 2020. This supplemented parallel downslides in lending rates from 2011 onwards. Such changes in China's monetary policy, covering variations in interest rates, CRRs as well as depreciated exchange rate, were all synchronized to achieve the targeted 'domestic circulation', with international circulation in its support from outside.

The impact of the changing currency management in China that started in 2005 was considerably moderated by the time of the recent shift in priorities in China, including the shift from international to domestic circulation in terms of the dual circulation policy. Its relevance for domestic firms in China was evident in statements as by Andrew Weir of KPMG Hong Kong: 'Where linkages with the global economy create vulnerabilities, China wants to minimize them.' Further, 'Where the linkages create benefits, China wants to expand them.'[81]

AGGREGATE FLOWS OF FINANCE TO THE REAL ECONOMY: CALCULATIONS BY THE CENTRAL BANK OF CHINA

According to estimates made by China's central bank of the *aggregate flow of finance to the real economy*, the flow has been increasing, especially in years like 2020[82] which was subject to the pandemic and in the long years of declining GDP growth rates since the GFC. The pattern as above for China is distinctly unique as compared to what was experienced by a large number of developing countries having financial booms along with real stagnation.

TABLE 4.1 *Flows of finance to the real economy* in RMB bn

2019	307041
2020	614082
2021	313408
2022	320099

Source: http://www.pbc.gov.cn/en/3688247/3688975/4787948/4787989/index.html

It thus appears from the above that China, continuing with accommodative expansionary policies, in effect attempted to instil an expansionary process in its domestic economy to take care of geopolitical contractions, especially during 2020.

SECTOR-WISE SHARES IN CHINA'S GDP

As the high growth phase in China came to an end during the global financial crisis, the relative size of the contribution from industry to GDP in the country was on further decline, especially as compared to the contribution of services. By 2020, with agriculture's contribution to GDP at less than 10 per cent, the share of the services sector, subject to further uptrends, exceeded 50 per cent of the aggregate contributions to the GDP. The recession in the west, including in the US, affected the downslides in the growth rate as well as the share of industry in China's GDP. The changing direction of the shares of the three major sectors of the Chinese economy in the country's GDP were affected further in recent years by geopolitical and health-related developments including the war in Eurasia and the pandemic.

The rising share of the services sector in China's GDP reflects the growing integration of China's domestic economy with the global market. This has been responsible for related expansions in China's financial activities as well as in services like transportation and shipping services, domestic trade, hotel and catering services, and real estate.

It is however worth noting that the increase in the share of the services sector in the GDP of China did not imply a higher GDP growth rate. The reasons include the predominance of financial services, especially in speculation, casting adverse effects on the real estate market and its downturns. This was especially true between 2005 and 2020.

Similar was the case for the lower GDP growth of the country over the long period of lockdown in the major metropolitan

FIGURE 4.21 *Sector-wise shares in GDP of China* in percentages

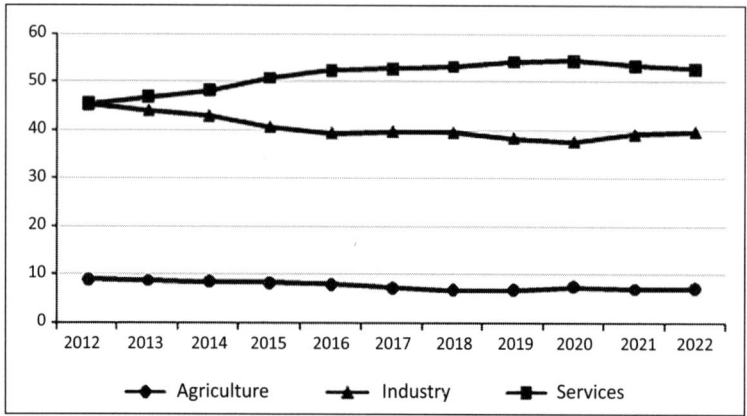

Source: National Bureau of Statistics of China, available at https://www.statista.com/statistics/270325/distribution-of-gross-domestic-product-gdp-across-economic-sectors-in-china

areas of China, which were subject to a zero-tolerance policy for Covid-19 in early 2022.

It however remains true that with state regulations continuing at least in the background, China's financial sector, despite the larger contribution to services and GDP, did not get the push to become the most dominant and powerful sector in the economy. This made the pattern in China very different from that in other EMEs.

MANAGING ECONOMIC POLICIES

China faced serious instabilities after the RMB was delinked, in 2015 at the end of a long period, from its fixed rate of 8.24 RMB per dollar and allowed to float. The fixed rate, till then subject to control by the PBoC, faced a major break when its floating in the market led to an appreciation over the next few years. This was largely caused by the steadily rising inflows of short-term portfolio capital, which continued over most of the years between 2007 and 2020 with expectations of further appreciation of the RMB. Short-term inflows and outflows were mostly in search of speculation-led operations in the currency market. It was rather a surprise that gross FDI inflows were also subject to volatility when the currency was floated, which in all probability was induced by the rise in speculation in China's capital market.

The changes in capital flows also led the REER (based on consumer prices relating to a four-currency basket, as mentioned above) to move up from 84.9 in 2005 to 130.05 in 2015 (Figure 4.17), having some adverse effects on China's trade balance by losing competitiveness. Appreciation of the nominal exchange rate and REER over 2005 and 2014 were opposed to China's pursuit, from 2020, of maintaining a depreciated currency as part of the package of an expansionary strategy, especially under Xi Jinping. This, however, has been followed by frequent depreciations in the following years till the present, ensuring the expansionary process in terms of the dual circulation policy.

Deviation from the expansionary strategy and the related stress due to instabilities in the financial sector reappeared when some more changes in currency management were initiated by policymakers in China, which were often responsible for increased speculation. The three measures (mentioned earlier) included: (1) introduction of universal banking in 2005, permitting banks to invest in security markets; (2) two-way floating of the RMB in 2011, causing further currency speculation; and (3) widening of the daily trading limit of the RMB against the dollar in 2012, leading to further currency speculation. The result was a downward slide of the RMB from 2014, subject to temporary breaks – of course a move which suited the expansionary strategy well, but probably at some cost of financial stability.

At the end of 2005, when the currency had started floating, policymakers in China sought to arrest the appreciated nominal rate as well as the REER of the RMB by sterilizing the excess supply of foreign currency. This was done by selling domestic currency for dollars in the market. The added supply of domestic currency which entered the economy as a result was however considered by the Chinese monetary authorities as *the cause for the rise in prices*, as in mainstream *quantity theory of money*. This was a *deviation of official policy in the direction of neoliberal economics*, away from the Keynesian move prevailing in their dual circulation strategy.

Here, we would like to mention an earlier study[83] where we had put to test the relationship between the changes in China's money supply (M2) due to dollar purchases from the market, and changes in the official reserves between 2006 and 2010. We also tested the effects of the sterilization policies on price stability.

Our empirical exercise reflected some positive changes in both M2 and the stock of official reserves ('high-powered money'), as was to be expected. Since the latter was considered to cause expansions in money supply, official policies were implemented in China to tighten credit – following the *principles of inflation-targeting* as under neoliberalism. This was done by pushing up the lending rate of interest from 2005 to 2007 (Figure 4.20), by raising CRRs, and by selling bonds against the RMB through open market operations (OMOs). By doing this China deviated temporarily from Keynesian expansionary policies and resorted to inflation-targeting – a move that clearly was contrary to the otherwise defiant pace of monetary policy in the country. The move was to address the excess flows of short-term capital under deregulated finance. We also notice instabilities in China's financial market which affected the stock exchange, whose genesis can be traced back to successive stages of deregulation in the financial sector.

Thus China's integration with the global economy brought with it a series of vulnerabilities, including a drop in its trade surplus and volatile exchange rate movements. These played a direct role in initiating a downslide in the country's GDP growth rate between 2007 and 2020. The expansionary monetary-fiscal policies which started at the end of the GFC of 2008–09 however continued, supported later by a depreciating exchange rate from 2014.

Of course, China has always been in a position to use official controls over the financial market to mitigate the destabilizing consequences. Policymakers in China were also in a relatively better position to gain from the geopolitical benefits of the Belt and Road Initiative, BRICS, and trade and investment prospects.

On the whole, financial reforms in China (especially the moves towards deregulation) initially had the effect of initiating both uncertainty and volatility in the market. Financial liberalization, which was in accord with the global move to open up markets, also had an impact on the Chinese state's surveillance over the economy. To some extent this was reflected in the deviations mentioned above, which led the monetary authorities to use standard tools of the monetarist 'inflation-targeting' strategy (like the lending rate, the CRR and open market operations) to control credit flows. The temporary decline in the capacity of the state to control the financial market can be witnessed in the tussle – for example, with the busting of the stock market bubble in 2015, when the state failed in its attempt to arrest collapse in the market. Similar instances of instability in the financial sector, surfacing in stock markets, currency speculation and, of late, in the real estate market, have also not always met with effective stabilization at the behest of the state. These instances of relative instability in China's financial sector could even provide a counterpoint to the potentials of an expansionary 'dual circulation' strategy which has been operative since 2020.

Situations as above of instability in the financial market and related declines in GDP growth rate led China to move to the dual circulation policy of Xi Jinping which, as mentioned above, was officially endorsed in July 2020. *The expansionary strategy adopted by China to boost its domestic economy asserted, in effect, a resolve on its part to reduce dependence on the rest of the world and to steer economic policies in that direction.*

By following the new strategy, China has been seeking to withstand the pressures from externally determined changes on her domestic policies, and to more or less maintain autonomy in deciding on *rates of interest*, the *exchange rate* and the *level of fiscal expenditure* as were appropriate for its economy. This has been especially consistent with the country's official pledge to prioritize domestic circulation and to move away from the previous strategy of export-oriented growth.

Debates on the State of the Chinese Economy

There have been ongoing debates among those researching the current state of China's economy. Pessimistic positions, including those coming from the World Bank,[84] downgrade the predicted growth rate of the economy for 2024 from 4.8 per cent to 4.4 per cent. This is in line with similar other positions pointing to the real estate crash and defaults, especially by the company Evergrande.

Among the reasons cited for the downslide in China's growth rate, the demographic policy of 'one child' of the 1980s is often held responsible for the related housing crisis in the the country. Daniel Gros, apprehending possible protectionary steps from the west, considers the surplus savings and current account surpluses of China as potential results of the above situation. The argument also relates to the IMF's prediction that GDP growth in China will reach just 4.5 per cent in 2024 and decline to 3 per cent by the end of this decade. As held by Gros, 'China would then have to maintain a current-account surplus of ten percentage points of GDP to keep its economy in equilibrium. At nearly $2 trillion, that would be enough to affect the global savings/investment balance.'[85]

There are others, however, with an optimistic outlook regarding the Chinese economy's prospects in the coming years, who consider the state to be a major plank of the process.[86] The *South China Morning Post* reported, 'China's economic prospects are brighter than they appear. Consumption was the main driver of Chinese growth in 2023, accounting for 82.5 per cent of the increase in GDP.' Further, 'China remains well-positioned to achieve much higher growth than most developed economies. The key is to move away from its conservative approach over the past decade, towards expansion.'

Keyu Jin, an academic from London, states that 'the American campaign to limit Chinese firms' access to critical technologies back-fired, motivating China to become technologically self-reliant.'[87] She adds that there are no signs 'that China is moving toward greater capital-account liberalization. On the contrary, growing economic and geopolitical uncertainty may prompt China to tighten its capital accounts.'[88]

The optimism is shared by Yu Yongding of the Institute for World Economics and Politics (IWEP), at the Chinese Academy of Social Sciences(CASS). In a recent post, he makes the point that China's GDP growth, which tapered down to 4.35 per cent in Q1 of 2023, could rise further to 6 per cent, provided the deficient demand could be met.[89] The process may be helped by the 'inward-looking policy' which relies on the home market, as is consistent with Xi Jinping's 'dual circulation' policy.

Yongding had echoed the same prediction in his earlier posts while approving the suggested route of expansionary policies. As he pointed out, with inflation at moderate or low levels and the rate of growth tapering off, there needs to be fiscal and monetary expansion to achieve higher growth.

Commenting further on China's encounters with global integration, Yongding clarifies that the 'dual circulation' strategy with its emphasis on the domestic market does *not* imply 'autarchy'. Instead, it is a new development strategy with which China has responded to western antagonism. While continuing to 'engage with global markets and supply chains, she will rely on domestic markets rather than external demand to drive economic growth'.[90] This is clearly very different from the current concerns in the west about 'comprehensiveness'.

We also mention here the official pronouncements of the Communist Party of China in their recently held plenum of July 2024. Among the 'big changes', a majority approved a document laying out a plan for 'deepening reform' and advancing 'Chinese-style modernization', according to the state media.[91] According to Chinese sources, 'To invoke Socialism with Chinese Characteristics is to remind cadres that China follows a distinct path to modernity. This path not only precludes the wholesale importation of Western institutions and values, but also provides an explanation for perceived Western hostility to China's National Rejuvenation'.[92]

As reported, it entails promoting consumption 'the Chinese way' with social safety nets including insurance, unemployment, health care, retirement, etc., 'to induce households to save less and spend more', rather than increasing disposable income as wages which goes against export competitiveness. The measures focus on public provisions to increase aggregate consumption by targeting the low retail sales of 2 per cent which pulled down growth in Q2 GDP to less than 4.7 per cent.[93]

As held by the plenum in 2024, the three pillars for deepening reforms and pursuing modernization, and to remain important as growth drivers, are consumption, green energy and innovation.[94] The positive outlook of the new approach of Xi Jinping, and its remodelling in the context of a low growth rate caused by low consumption, is likely to produce an added degree of sustainability by instituting reforms for 'socialism with Chinese characteristics'. The new approach promotes egalitarian measures to raise consumption without having to raise wages, which is considered to hamper export-competitiveness. However, it does not preclude possible chaos and downturns which may be faced by China, especially given the prevailing churns on the geopolitical scene. Those include the current tariff escalations and trade war launched by US President Trump, having no direction whatsoever. This confirms that the future is always unpredictable, to repeat what Keynes professed in his famous statement: 'about those matters, we do not know'. No prediction on this matter can also be made of the future course of the Chinese economy especially, in the absence of a consideration of the dynamics of the geopolitical factors which are beyond any prediction.

In Conclusion: The Asian Economies

We may conclude this chapter on the Asian EMEs with the observation that financial liberalization had much to do with the intermittent crises faced by these economies in their financial markets, which even led to stagnation of their real economies. This, however, has been denied by the proponents of mainstream economics, who continue to have a major role in shaping official policies in the majority of the subordinated developing countries which include the Asian EMEs. The proven failures of open financial markets, which became evident in the unsuccessful attempts to contain the GFC beyond its origin in the US, have been ineffective to provide a lesson, and even to policymakers in the advanced economies who are still busy continuing remedial measures along the same lines. Thus, according to Ben Bernanke, who was in charge of the US Federal Reserve during the global crisis, much of it was due to 'credit market disruptions' with banks having a role in handling credit supply with risks.[95] Explanations such as these reflect a supply-based narrative which fitted well with the neoliberal remedial measures that followed, including those that attempted to bail out the stressed entities like big banks with little concern for deeper issues.

We considered, to provide an example of a line of thinking that was similar, the views of Raghuram Rajan who held the top position in the Reserve Bank of India between 2013 and 2016. While having differences with the Indian government on the autonomy of the bank and related matters, Rajan had a rather condescending attitude to ongoing practices in the financial sector, despite what he observed as the 'perverse' behaviour of bank managers in concealing risks from investors by moving away asset prices from what he continued to believe were 'fundamentals'.[96]

In EMEs like India, no serious attempt has been made at the official level – not even under someone like RBI Governor Y.V. Reddy who dealt with the 2008 crisis in a heroic manner – to mend the glitches in the economy caused by deregulated finance and financialization especially over 2005 to 2019. The same is true of China, as can be seen with the Chinese state making hardly any attempt to comprehend the pejorative consequences of deregulated finance and financialization. Finally, in the Latin American EMEs, as can be expected with the rulings conducted by the established elites in their official positions in those countries having close links to global finance, there has never been any sign of an attempt to reverse the onslaught and capture of finance over their real economies.

The EMEs we have discussed in this chapter share, in principle rather than in practice, some concern for meeting the minimal requirements for subsistence and survival of the majority of their population who have been solely dependent on the limited opportunities available in those stagnating economies. The responsibility for ameliorating issues such as above is inevitably sidetracked by the ruling governments, which are most often run by the rich and powerful who stand to gain by the triumph of finance and financialization. The underlying logic and its history will be dealt with in chapter 5 which follows.

NOTES

[1] Mani (2012).

[2] Sen (2008).

[3] Ibid.

[4] Sen and Dasgupta (2014); also see Sen (2019).

[5] The primary budget is arrived at by deducting interest payments from the fiscal budget.

[6] Sen (2019).

[7] See 'Narasimham Committee Reports', available at https://www. scribd.com/presentation/250848882/Narasimham-Committee-Reports.

[8] Sen and Dasgupta (2023).

[9] Gottschalk and Sen (2010).

[10] Sen and Ghosh (2005).

[11] See https://tejimandi.com/blogs/tm-learn/fiis-impact-on-the-indian-stock-market.

[12] Sen and Vaidya (1997).

[13] https://americandeposits.com/history-quantitative-easing-united-states/.

[14] Mundell (1960); see also, Fleming (1962).

[15] Sen and Dasgupta (2014).

[16] Expenditure in primary budget is fiscal expenditure less interest payments.

[17] Urjit Patel Report on Monetary Policy Reform, 2014; S. Chakravarty Report on Working of Monetary System, 1982.

[18] Rajan (2017), p. 75.

[19] Ibid.

[20] Sriram, ed. (2018), pp. 80–84.

[21] Ibid.

[22] 'Report of the Committee on Financial Inclusion 2008' (chaired by Rangarajan), p. 90.

[23] Sriram, ed. (2018), p. 90.

[24] 'India Weighted Average Lending Rates', available at https://trading economics.com/india/bank-lending-rate#.

[25] Aizenman and Lee (2007).

[26] Reserve Bank of India (RBI), *Handbook of Statistics for the Indian Economy*, 1990–2024.

[27] As mentioned already, capital gains and losses arising from transactions of financial assets are never a part of the GDP, as held in standard national accounting practices.

[28] Sen and Dasgupta (2018).

[29] Reserve Bank of India (RBI) Bulletins, 1990–2017.

[30] Dasgupta and Raghavendra (2024).

[31] See Bose and Kumar (2018).

[32] Reserve Bank of India (RBI), *Handbook of Statistics for the Indian Economy*, 1990–2024.

[33] See Sen (2023c), pp. 468–73.

[34] Sen (2021a).

[35] *Economic Survey 2023–24*, cited in *The Hindu*, 22 July 2024.

[36] See Sen (2023b) for analysis.

[37] For a broad review, see Kumar (2021).

[38] Primary budget = fiscal budget less interest payments.

[39] *Economic Survey 2025–26*.

[40] See https://www.rbi.org.in/Scripts/PublicationsView.aspx?id=21134.

[41] Government of India (GoI) (2025).

[42] Wani (2025); see also Dhar (2025).

[43] Sen (2014a), p. 248.

[44] Ibid., p. 233.

[45] Ibid., pp. 237–39.

[46] Sen (2012).

[47] Sen, ed. (2014b), pp. 37–39.

[48] Nolan (2012), p. 70.

[49] See https://www.ft.com/content/c6440ddb-7052-3997-b29d-8f380f31 bdee.

[50] Sen (2007a), p. 238.

[51] Silver (2022); see also, Swanson (2019).

[52] See Giovannini (2020).

[53] Ibid.

54 See 'China Savers Ignore Efforts to Cool $3 Trillion WMP Market', available at https://www.bloomberg.com/news/articles/2019-04-14/china-s-savers-ignore-efforts-to-cool-3-trillion-wmp-market.

55 Sen (2014b).

56 Sen (2021b), p. 261.

57 See www.news.xinhuanet.com/english/china/2012-04/14/c_131526335.htm. Also Gallagher *et al.*, eds (2014), pp. 80–81.

58 See People's Bank of China, Finance Survey and Statistics Department, 13 February and 17 April 2012, http://www.pbc.gov.cn/en/3688066/3688080/index.html.

59 Zhang (2014).

60 Sen (2014b); also see Sen (2013).

61 See 'China: Foreign Exchange Reserves', available at https://tradingeconomics.com/china/foreign-exchange-reserves.

62 Yongding (2012).

63 Sen (2013).

64 Ibid.

65 Sen (2021b).

66 Sen (2014b).

67 https://www.statista.com/statistics/458189/china-stock-market-total-market-capitalization/.

68 https://tradingeconomics.com/china/stock-market.

69 See 'China: Foreign Exchange Reserves', https://tradingeconomics.com/china/foreign-exchange-reserves.

70 Yongding (2019).

71 See https://www.bloomberg.com/quote/USDCNY:CUR.

72 See 'Dual Circulation at Heart of Economic Strategy', available at https://english.www.gov.cn/news/topnews/202103/05/content_WS60418456c6d0719374af9ff8.html.

73 Lubin (2022).

74 Ibid.

75 See http://www.pbc.gov.cn/en/.

76 Yao (2020).

77 See 'Will the Dual Circulation Strategy Enable China to Compete in a Post-Pandemic World?', https://chinapower.csis.org/china-covid-dual-circulation-economic-strategy/. Also see, He (2023).

78 iitf.org/publications/2024/08/19/how-innovative-is-China-in-semiconductors

79 https://americandeposits.com/history-quantitative-easing-united-states/.

80 https://www.ceicdata.com/en/indicator/china/reserve-requirement-ratio.

81 https://kpmg.com/cn/en/home/ html.

82 See http://www.pbc.gov.cn/en/3688247/3688975/4787948/4787989/index.html.

83 Sen (2014a), pp. 263–300.

84 Coy (2023).

85 Gros (2023).

86 Yongding (2024a).

87 Jin (2023).

88 Ibid.

89 Yongding (2023a).

90 See Yongding (2023a, 2023b, 2023c, 2023d, 2024a).

91 See http://www.pbc.gov.cn/en/3688247/3688975/4787948/4787989/index.html

92 https://www.strategictranslation.org/glossary/socialism-with-chinese-characteristics. Also see Bukowski *et al.* (2024).

93 Ibid.

94 Tran (2024).

95 Bernanke (2020).

96 Rajan (2017).

5

Subordination in Developing Economies
Economic and Socio-Political Context

SUBORDINATION IN THE NEO-COLONIES OF THE PERIPHERY

The Modalities of Subordination

The majority of countries in the global South, often identified as the 'periphery', experienced over a long time a subordinate status in relation to overseas countries most of which exercised political domination over them through colonial rule. The political control as exercised by those colonizing countries was their major tool to extract financial resources, and to appropriate export earnings as well as local tax revenues, from the colonized countries. Such a pattern prevailed in India under the British rule during the late nineteenth and early twentieth centuries, and the appropriations that took place, as mentioned above, were legitimately described by contemporary nationalists as the 'drain of resources'.[1]

Transfers from the peripheral countries are still continuing, but they have gone through major transformations in terms of the mode of appropriation. In a large number of countries which gained their political independence in the post-war years, a state of surveillance continued to be exercised by their previous colonizers, which include the advanced economies of today. Those erstwhile colonizers have acquired the power to monitor as well as control the official policies in countries of the periphery, which in effect has turned them into *subordinated neo-colonies*.

By initiating the opening up of markets in those economies through commands which were often discreet and indirectly communicated across countries, the advanced nations made use of the liberalized markets to operate as agents for corporates and other institutions overseas to transfer profits and other income from the subordinated countries by using channels of trade and finance.

Conceptual Tools to Identify Subordination

The notion of subordination, in a broader context, was originally formulated by Antonio Gramsci, Italian intellectual, philosopher and politician,[2] who defined it as a system of class alliance in which the 'hegemonic class' exercised political leadership over 'subaltern classes' by 'winning them over'. Formulated in the context of what he observed as the colonization of southern Italy by the northern part of the country, he used 'hegemony' to imply economic leadership – besides ethical leadership. Making use of the above notions, Gramsci provided an early formulation of his elaborate concept of power.[3] As held by him, hegemony entails for a class its execution of a leadership role on the economic, political, moral and intellectual levels vis-à-vis other classes in the system.

Elaborations of Gramsci's formulations include comments that, by possessing hegemony, the ruling class uses culture to maintain power and wealth; also that the process requires use of ideology rather than force to maintain power. It is held that the ideas and values embodied in culture are often expressed in terms of control over institutions, with the media, universities and religious institutions being used to reproduce hegemony.[4] In our view, the above narrative captures well the current subordination of emerging economies by hegemonic powers from abroad.

While economic subordination and the use of hegemonic power to implement it can be considered the major theme of analysis in this book, we also recognize the role of the state at different stages of the opening up of the market and its facilitation, in particular by changing the legal and institutional set-up within countries. We also show, later in this chapter, how social norms have simultaneously played a supportive role to the liberalization of markets by initiating commercialization of all transactions. The basic idea behind all the above can certainly be linked to Gramsci's notion of subordinated categories (for us, countries in the global South), which are dominated by the hegemonic powers, currently of rich nations in the global North.

On Economic Subordination in the Periphery

The ongoing phase of economic subordination in the periphery relies on the supportive ideology of 'neoliberalism' as identified by heterodox economists. We outline this here in brief detail, in continuation of what has been narrated in earlier chapters.

Accepted as a cure-all by the stagflation-affected countries of Western Europe in the mid-1970s, neoliberalism gained further acceptance when sophisticated mathematical tools emerged to evaluate financial assets in the market. One can refer, in particular, to the Black-Scholes options pricing model which has been widely used to calculate returns on stocks.[5] There was also a claim in neoliberal analysis that 'financial repression' resulting from controls can be held responsible for prevailing inefficiencies in markets having low risk–low returns on investments.[6]

The financial sectors of most nations witnessed a sea-change in their *mode of intermediation* under financial liberalization. This included shifting a large part of financial transactions from direct control of banks to markets, a distinct change from the 'visible hand' of relationship banking to the axiomatic 'invisible hand' that is supposed to be anonymous and self-regulating. With finance-friendly policies in the market, there were reduced levels of controls over cross-border capital transactions, which went with the pumping in of additional liquidity in domestic stock markets, accompanying reduced levels of taxation of wealth and capital gains.

In mainstream economics, the superiority of a 'market-based' financial system rests on Friedrich Hayek's claim that 'the market is an *omniscient way of knowing*,'[7] in particular one that radically exceeds the capacity of any individual mind or even the state.[8] But, as argued from heterodox quarters, the Hayekian view ignores the 'social aspects of finance', and their impact on financial institutions and on income and wealth distribution. With capital account liberalization, the demands from richer households for high risk–high return, triple-A rating financial assets are often met and transacted by foreign institutional investors (FIIs). In this process, the regulation of finance and related matters by the state remains contested under contemporary capitalism in spite of the fact that regulations can play an important role in structuring capital accumulation and distribution in capitalist economies.[9]

Expropriating the neo-colonies by making use of liberalized markets has proved rewarding for the advanced economies, in particular by providing support to their stagnating economies at the time the 'golden age' of capitalism came to a close in the mid-1970s. In the peripheral economies, the market reached a commanding height during the early years of globalization in the early 1990s along with the integration of countries and liberalization. The state was gradually pushed to the backstage in terms of most of its earlier roles other than its actively facilitating the liberalization of the market. Once the process of liberalizing the market was initiated, some requisite changes were implemented in the domestic financial institutions, mostly in conformity with the Washington consensus from the Bretton Woods institutions.

Neither the policies prescribed by the state nor the institutional changes that came up were of advantage to the periphery. Examples include the IMF loans offered to mitigate the currency crises faced by some of the developing nations with conditionality based on monetarist policies and austerity. These loans also catered to further liberalization of markets as well as exchange rate flexibility in the borrowing countries.

From Dependency to Economic Subordination

The opening up of markets as a condition for the grant of loans, as with loans from the IMF or corporate financial institutions, signified an end to the era of *dependency*, when countries could rely official loans or aid from overseas bilateral sources to meet deficits in external payments. Funds released as loans under official development assistance (ODA) were often tied to purchases from the creditor country, making it difficult for the borrowing economy to settle its debt charges, which were often in hard currency like the US dollar.[10] This added to further problems for the receiving countries. By the early 1980s, countries in the periphery were faced with limited options for availing official loans in times of need. This came about due to the limited availability of ODA from recession-prone OECD (Organization for Economic Cooperation and Development) countries.

The developing countries encountered a severe debt crisis in the early 1980s, caused by a crash in the global commodity market and a stiff upturn in interest rates in the US, which pushed up the charges on their outstanding debts from overseas. The crisis led some of those countries to approach the IMF for loans, which came with conditionalities that included a strict time frame for the opening up of their markets. Loans with similar conditionalities were received by India and some other developing countries, opening the floodgates of market liberalization.

During the debt crisis of the early 1980s as well as in the early 1990s, the IMF was advancing loans with strict conditionalities. This was followed, almost immediately, by the simultaneous integration (globalization) and liberalization of markets in most developing countries. With liberalized markets in place, the modality of subordination could be easily worked out in these countries, whereby the market operated as an agent for creditors including overseas corporates. As mentioned earlier, the market had the power to stall any attempt on the part of the host country to deviate from liberalization of credit flows. This also ensured the process of continuing expropriation from the periphery.

In contrast to the earlier pattern of *expropriation by official creditors under dependency*, there emerged under *subordination a new pattern of expropriation initiated by overseas corporate finance from private sources*. The arrangement was backed by the compliance of both the state and the big (*comprador*) bourgeoisie in the receiving countries, with both having an alliance with overseas capital. By using the market as an agency to operate on behalf of the creditors both from transnational corporations (TNCs) and multinational banks from the advanced economies, they ushered in an *alternate process of surplus transfer from those peripheral neo-colonies subject to economic subordination*.

It may be mentioned here that the *distinction* drawn above, between the phases of dependence and of subordination, is generally *missed out* in the literature on related issues.[11] It also bears reiteration here that while situations of dependence and subordination both entailed costs to the host economies in the periphery, transfers of surpluses through the market under economic subordination made the *receiving nations pass through a different experience by involving in it, their social and political processes*. Under colonialism, as well as with dependence (on overseas loans), expropriation of surpluses involved the *direct use of political power*. In contrast, under subordination surpluses are appropriated by the so-called *invisible hand* of the market itself, operating on behalf of its clients overseas. They include the big financial corporates and banks in alliance with the state and the club of powerful institutions in the host region.

Economic policies in the receiving countries under subordination usually go by mainstream neoliberal principles as are usually adhered to by overseas official and private agencies. As mentioned, often, the host country governments along with big (comprador) business at home share some mutual interest with overseas institutions and governments – streamlining further the path of expropriation by the market.

We point out again that the pattern of subordination in the countries of the periphery did not prevail when they were under post-war dependency. Unlike in the past when official bilateral loans or grants imposed a direct state of dependency on the part of the state in the receiving country vis-à-vis the donor, policies now adopted in subordinated economies cater to a much wider circle of beneficiaries, including the large transnational corporates in finance and industry from the global North as a whole.

The Role of the State in Subordinated Economies

A lot of changes have taken place in the *role of the state* in subordinated economies. Of those, a major one has been the initiative by the state to introduce *universal banking* in these economies. The integration of global financial markets which had taken place under globalization brought pressure on the state, especially from corporate finance, to allow banks to have access to security markets, which was finally made possible under universal banking. The facility to transact securities generated more income for banks from security transactions as compared to what was received from traditional deposit banking. Simultaneously, the newly opened opportunities for overseas capital flows, especially short-term ones, led to those inflows being multiplied and channelized towards the rejuvenated security market with the participation of banks – often with fiscal impunity.

Under universal banking, financial intermediation by banks and other financial institutions marked a distinctive shift, away from the 'visible hand' of relationship banking (under segregated banking) to the axiomatic 'invisible hand' of the market which, in mainstream economics, was considered anonymous and self-regulating.[12]

Institutional changes in the subordinated countries also included promotion, by the state in large numbers of EMEs and other developing countries, of their stock exchanges. Stock exchange activities got a fillip when large inflows of short-term portfolio capital by FIIs were allowed to enter the stock market. The entry of FIIs into the stock market was a sequel to universal banking entailing transactions in securities, most often in the form of short-term capital flows transacted in the stock exchange.

The stock market in these economies under universal banking, unlike in the earlier years when credit was mostly available as loans from banks, was activated as a second channel for credit, while banks continued with their relatively limited scale of intermediation. The growing capitalization of the stock market in the EMEs was matched by rising short-term capital flows – with both having a close link to the wave of speculation and uncertainty resulting from financial liberalization.

STRUCTURAL CHANGES: THE RISE OF FINANCE TO DOMINANCE

We have already referred, in earlier chapters, to the significant structural changes which have taken place in some of the EMEs over the past few decades. Those changes include the rise of the services sector, which in most cases has moved up to the top in terms of its share in the GDP, to 50 per cent or more, especially since the onset of the global crisis in 2008. Financial activities, as mentioned, remain a major component of the services sector, more so because of its high-value transactions. As we mentioned, finance with its predominant share as high-value financial services, is a major contributor to GDP growth. While it cannot be denied that historically the power wielded by the financial sector increased with its *quantitative significance* to the GDP, the rise of finance to a position of dominance was actually made possible by the *qualitative valour* imparted by the political and social environment prevailing in those economies, which is discussed below. It was a combination of the above two aspects which worked to make finance the dominating sector with its capacity to control policies that could bring maximum benefits to itself. Changes such as above initiated a different era of *finance-led stagnation*, leaving far behind industrialization and the developmental state as alternate strategies.

We may cite here an observation that the rise of finance and its supremacy in the west was 'enabled by the confluence of a supportive ideology which had its *three planks* (including) of neoliberalism, historical circumstances like the "stagflation" of the 1970s and the development of sophisticated mathematical tools for valuing financial assets like the Black-Scholes options pricing model'.[13] The pattern was more or less similar across the subordinated countries of the global South. We also recount here the fact that finance in liberalized markets has an in-built mechanism which can stall any turn in policies away from liberalization, by posing the threat of a reversal of capital flows. This worked well to channelize policies in capital-importing countries in a direction that favoured finance in particular.

Further, the state in these countries sought to minimize its role by privatizing publicly owned units of business, which follows from the neoliberal principles of market efficiency, with consequences that are often detrimental in terms of social benefits or even growth. Structural changes in a subordinated country did need *the active support of the ruling state*, which had little interest to try out alternatives that could benefit its home economy.

Dominant Finance in Subordinate Economies: The Underlying Political and Social Contexts

For most countries in the developing region, which include the EMEs, the rise in power enjoyed by the financial sector has relied not just on the massive and growing scale of financial transactions in recent times, but also on the political and social environments[14] within the country in support of such power.

Interpretations in the literature which seek to identify the primary causes behind the *expansionary process of finance* come from *two opposite positions*. In the *mainstream* view, the explanation for the expansion of financial activities includes: (1) advances in mainstream financial theory; (2) developments in information and communications technology (ICT); and (3) deregulation of financial markets.[15]

This view has been *contested by heterodox analysts*[16] who argue that interpretations relying on methodological individualism in mainstream economic theory *ignore the political and social implications* of the expanding financial sector. For example, technological innovations mostly have their origin in specifically defined problems of large firms alone, which are usually located in advanced economies. The process can never retain neutrality, given their final use by big capital. The heterodox critics also argue that mainstream theories have consistently ignored such aspects by treating technological developments (including the internet) as *fortuitous changes* which helped financialization.

The heterodox position further points out that the precise sources and mechanisms of the influence of the financial sector over the policymaking process include 'three basic types of power: *instrumental, ideological and structural* … a combination of which allows the financial sector to secure formidable leverage over political outcomes' (emphasis added).[17] Further interpretations are there along the same lines which identify the *instrumental* dimension as 'conscious and formal political activity by financial actors, their institutions and associations'. We may relate this to our analysis of the alliance between the state and financial institutions on steps for further liberalization like universal banking. As further mentioned in the literature,

Ideological power refers to the overarching neoliberal policy consensus among senior elements of the corporate and political worlds (including media) ... closely aligned with major financial institutions and investors who benefit immensely from the opening up of new market opportunities – through privatization, an anti-inflationary fiscal policy and the implementation of austerity that shifts the burden of post-crisis adjustment upon the population.[18]

Once again it is not difficult to trace the bonding of *ideological* and neoliberal principles which facilitated major turns towards the financialization of economies as discussed in earlier chapters.

Finally, the *structural aspects* as a basic source of power refers to 'the persistent threat of capital flight and capital relocation that hangs over public representatives when making delicate choices about the conduct of economic policy'.[19] This has been evident in the continuation of neoliberal policies in subordinated economies which have no autonomy over their domestic economic policies.

Processes such as detailed above are not difficult to locate in both the advanced countries and the developing countries. As an example, we may look at the systematic *dismantling of regulatory frameworks*, actual or proposed, which has been operational in the USA during the years following the global financial crisis. With Donald Trump's first term as president of the US from 2017 to 2021 and later his second term in 2025, the ideological leanings came to the fore clearly. Earlier than that, the Dodd–Frank Wall Street Reform and Consumer Protection Act of 2010 was dismantled by Trump despite its attempts to protect the public against future financial speculation as happened during the GFC.[20] The story has evolved further in ongoing manoeuvres led by Trump in his capacity as a re-elected president in 2025. For instance, his mercantilist command over tariff policies to 'make America great again' (MAGA) and strictures on immigrants which fail to realize that the age of mercantilism was different from the present period, and that possible trade wars may completely overturn the norms that so far prevailed in geopolitics. Trump may not be close to the mainstream position nor in favour of the opposite arguments on state policy, but his actions certainly reflect the relevance of state power in framing policies which are far from what is required.

As heterodox economists point out, changes in the global political environment as above have generated a new category of investors, *corporate managers,* who are expected to shorten their time horizons and disburse company profits through stock buybacks and the issuing of dividends, *all at the expense of re-investments* in real terms.[21] We can recall here how the managers invest in speculation-led financial securities when a part of their salary comes in the form of employee stock ownership plans (ESOPs), which lead them to buy company stocks and raise their prices.

For the heterodox school, this increase in compensation is a *prime example* of the ongoing 'shareholder value' ideology which, as mentioned, has been least beneficial for further investment in the real economy.[22] The norm followed to achieve *maximum shareholder value* has been treated by the mainstream school as a core principle for operations among financial actors.[23] The use of ESOPs as compensation for managers has led to the share prices of the company along with its balance sheet getting a boost, while the company experiences no expansion in real terms. Instead, there is an urge on the part of corporate managers to boost the financial asset prices of the company they work for, all in their own interest.[24] This entails *a change in priorities, with personal gain prevailing alongside relative profitability* in the market, which *reflects societal changes.*

The use of complicated regulatory processes involving recent innovations in the area of managerial finance has made public bodies (like corporates) ripe for regulatory capture by the financial sector, and created a demand to recruit private experts from this sector. As viewed by some,[25] this strengthens the 'revolving door' between financial and corporate organizations.[26]

Providing an example of the relevance of the above process

for the rise of the financial sector, we cite a study which offers a comprehensive analysis of a finance-related group identified as the 'Bankers' Club'. The collective has been investing huge sums of wealth in attaining *political power*, so that 'Wall Street owns most of Washington'.[27] As pointed out in the study, the non-financial corporates (NFCs) and financial corporates (FCs) continue to aspire to achieve their *common goal* of cheap labour with high productivity and weak bargaining power. It further observes that with stagnation and unemployment, technology has made it possible to achieve all the goals at one go as mentioned above.[28] In effect, the chief managing staff in the NFCs, which include their CEOs, have been subject to the impact of financialization which offers them investment opportunities in equities (as mentioned above, with ESOPs) having no contribution to expansion in real terms.[29]

The role of finance in transforming the economy and society,[30] as elaborated by heterodox economists,[31] also entails the *financialization of household income*. This is achieved through mortgages, car and housing loans, and even micro credit, the securitization of which under asset-based securities (ABSs) *is often carried forward as investment in the stock market*. Households are also participating indirectly in financial markets, often via investments of pension funds and insurance schemes. We may recall here the disastrous financial crisis of 2007–08, which was largely caused by the *use of derivatives with securitization of mortgaged assets* by investment banks, all with the connivance of the liberalized financial market!

Unlike in the period when investments were safe with moderate returns on bank deposits as their main channel, with financialization households have been enticed into making more money by investing in the stock market as well as in real estate. Such investments, while providing higher returns, are vulnerable to risk under layers of uncertainty with returns susceptible to further declines.

With financialization affecting households in developing countries, as we point out earlier in this book, one can notice the prevalence of *pre-capitalist relations* in the process of surplus extraction from households – a pattern that has been identified as *corporate feudalism*.[32] The pattern often emerges with an arrogation of coercive powers which earlier belonged only to the state. Examples include the use of private security to coerce defaulting households, which often oversteps the law of the country. The entry of households into financial markets also brings in additional risks connected with physical threats extended to borrowers. The passive attitude of the state in such matters reflects what can be identified as *an underlying alliance between the political process and the financial sector.*

Looking beyond the developing countries, the penetration of financial giants also had a major role in the economies of advanced countries, targeting households as easy prey for expropriation. A classic example, as mentioned above, of the disastrous consequences for the global economy was the sub-prime crisis with the US. Banks, generating assets with collateralized loans, targeting the low-income population in the country by offering cheap or sub-prime loans to purchase houses with mortgages. The scheduled payments were difficult to execute, due to both a drop in house prices and the loss of jobs faced by poor house owners. The rest is history: the major investment banks used ABSs to make profits, which culminated in a global crisis in financial markets, the GFC of 2008–09.[33] Banks, considered as 'too big to fail' (TBTF), were bailed out by the US treasury, which spent $700 billion to purchase the troubled assets of banks and other financial institutions. The shock, however, was critical for households that lost mortgaged property because they had no jobs to make payments; the losses were often equivalent to their life's savings.[34]

Opportunities such as above, of using low-income households to provide profits to banks and non-bank financial corporations (NBFCs), have now spread to the EMEs and other developing countries. This includes the incorporation of households into what can be described as 'circuits' of financialization, to which a typical method employed by the mega financial corporates has been the 'capture'[35] of households. With offers made for housing loans, credit cards, car loans, student loans and even micro-credit, corporate creditors make use of their power to extract penalties or even physical threats in case of defaults.[36]

The role of finance in the economy is often determined[37] by short-run capital flows which set the scale of liberalized financial transactions. The major source of those flows happens to be the foreign institutional investments (FIIs), which of late has become a powerful institution in most economies. Thus even with minor departures from the prevailing track of liberalization, there could be a reversal of the short-run inflows, which is often engineered by the FIIs. With the integration of economies under globalization it has thus become increasingly difficult for nations in the periphery to resist subordination by reinstituting controls on capital flows.

RESHAPING THE RULES OF THE GAME: FINANCIAL EXCLUSION AND UNEVEN DISTRIBUTION OF WEALTH

As pointed out,[38] 'finance is reshaping the rules of the game'. In effect, the financial industry, in terms of its size and power, is inseparably connected to the structural changes that simultaneously bring about rising income and wealth inequalities. Thus, richer households with a higher propensity to save are likely to hold their financial wealth as risky assets (such as mutual funds, shares and bonds). In the process, more money ends up in the hands of the management of institutional investors or 'asset managers' as well who handle these transactions.[39] Securitization of assets also fundamentally transforms the 'rules of the capitalist game',[40] and in rather perverse directions. As can be observed, with the expansion of finance which relies only on speculation, the demand for 'investment-grade' (AAA-rated) securities grows – and the result is a hunt for additional collaterals, akin to the pattern of the gold rush in earlier periods. It is held that 'obtaining collateral is similar to mining. It involves both exploration (looking for collateral deposits) and extraction (the "unearthing" of passive securities so they can be re-used as collateral for various purposes in the shadow banking system)'.[41] Thus, '... collateral is the new gold: this explains why banks [before the GFC] gave loans to non-credit-worthy (sub-prime) customers'.[42] That is also why these same banks are now eager to include the poor in the financial system,[43] and to encroach upon *ever-new spaces for profit-making.*[44]

Since financial exclusion is quite common when finance is liberalized, the earmarking of priority credit has been scrapped or modified in those markets (as in India). At the same time, with financialization the related transactions have reached new clients like households, who are approached with offers of consumer credit for car or housing loans. Also, banks have been securitizing the credit cards held by their clients, which are often households. This pattern is common in countries with an active asset-backed securitization (ABS) procedure. The securitization of financial assets has moved the transactions in a direction that is more unequal and, as pointed out, rather 'perverse'.[45]

Reshaping the 'rules of the game' has also affected corporate finance by making use of the employee stock ownership plans (ESOPs) paid to employees (especially to company managers), who tend to *repurchase* the company stocks to help raise prices of those stocks. The rise in stock prices turn out to be beneficial for the company managers with inflated receipts against their stock options or ESOPs. As pointed out, the process is certainly detrimental in terms of the potential investment in real assets for the company which could have taken place in the absence of the employees' involvement in stock trading. Such trading thus undermines, in aggregate, the real economy.[46]

Further on corporate finance, to meet current liabilities related to dividends and interest payments on past loans, the companies often need to borrow. This leads to a typically Minsky-type Ponzi situation with borrowings contributing to instability at the firm level if difficult to pay back, while failing to add to accumulation in the real economy. The emphasis on stock prices is often seen as a prime example of 'shareholder value' ideology, shared by corporate managers. Alternately, the pattern is viewed as the very essence of financialization which leads to 'short-termism'.[47]

The powerful status of mega financial units across the globe cannot continue in the absence of an explicit alliance between the ruling states of creditor countries and capital-importing countries in the periphery – an alliance often used to elicit mutual support for one another. It is not far-fetched to link the above to an underlying political leaning and a corresponding faith in mainstream economics which are shared both by the financial corporates and the ruling states. The alliance enabled the corporates to expand their scale of operations in the capital-importing countries by having access to production, advertising and use of media. The state in the host countries has been involved in changing institutions and the legal framework to work in favour of the corporate financial giants.

The mainstream school, however, denies criticisms such as above. They insist that the financial sector has the *power to transform*, not only the economy, but also the society and the political process of the developing nations. In support of this argument, it is pointed out that the markets for financial assets, especially in stock exchanges, have virtually changed the norms of investment for corporate investors by making it more profitable to invest in short-term financial assets – an act often referred to as 'share-holder primacy' on the part of corporate managers in the midst of the wave of financialization.[48]

THE POWER OF FINANCE AND
ITS LINKS TO THE POLITICAL PROCESS

We end this final chapter of the book by observing that the power acquired by the financial sector in subordinated economies, and especially in parliamentary democracies, relies considerably on the ongoing political process which is ready to provide facilitating measures. We here document some of these measures as shared by heterodox analysts.

For instance, the transfer of funds by FCs or NFCs to contesting parties at the time of elections, often on a discretionary basis, works as a big determining factor for political parties to win the election. The compensations continue as the party elected to power provides tax or other benefits to the donor companies, often violating the rules of law. Support such as above exchanged between the financial sector and the ruling state reflects their mutual interests and goals. It makes for proximity between the sources of finance and the prevailing political set-up, which in effect generates a cloud of 'political protection' for the financial industry. Such protection is reflected in the state permitting the defiance of regulatory actions without any accountability. Examples include, at a global scale: the gradual dilution of Basel norms; the bail-out of banks in the USA viewed as 'too big to fail' (TBTF); the rolling back, in 2018, of the Dodd–Frank Act in the US; and the rejection of the Financial Transaction Tax in the EU as well as in the UK. One can observe similar lapses in the developing countries, in the failure of official attempts to curb fraudulent transactions.

In most countries, despite having a government which is elected democratically under a parliamentary system, the party in power can continue despite the above lapses. This is possible because large numbers of citizens are either uninterested or are poorly informed about corrupt politics, or are even bribed to vote for the rich and the powerful (party) – a pattern which fails to convey policy preference through 'issue voting'.[49] In addition, there is increasingly the emergence of a new phenomenon of elected governments whose power emulates one-party dictatorships with absolute authority. Finance, of course, plays its role in providing support to such states, working in the mutual interest of the financial sector and the ruling state. Aspects such as above delineate clearly the helping hand lent to the ongoing political process by finance.

Financialization and Social Capital

Further empowerment of finance by enticing corporate managers and households to enter the risk-prone market for financial assets has been noticeable over some time. While political powers and the ruling state extended their passive approval to the new entrants into the circuit of speculatory finance due to its role in extending turnovers in the financial sector, there has been no concern for the instability and inequality that could result in the economy.[50] This point of view goes with a *societal change* that is characterized by the ready acceptance and approval of such situations in society.

Societal changes that have taken place with the rise of finance as the overpowering and dominant force in most countries can be traced to the decaying norms of 'social capital',[51] which, in earlier times, had a base in civic norms of reciprocity and generalized trust. These changes have left behind the shared values and networks, along with the institutions which facilitated cooperation and collective action for mutual benefit.[52] The result is obviously a sea-change in cultures and a big loss for humanity.

The evolving societal change was captured a long time ago by Karl Polanyi, who stated that as the sphere of the market is enlarged by capitalist expansion, it tends to destroy and *subordinate the social fabric* to standardized capitalist values embedded in the culture of the global market.[53] Polanyi further argued that this is achieved 'by violating the basic human nature ... [*as well as*] family, community and human relations. In terms of this position, unlimited expansion of the capitalist system along with the market ... are responsible for causing "dispossession, displacement and human degradation".[54] Nothing could be more vivid a description of the societal change than that offered by Polanyi's foresight more than six decades ago. However, his notion of 'double movement', whereby movements and protests of a discontented population are followed by countervailing forces with regenerative steps on the part of the state – to restore mutually supportive relations in the society[55] – is unrealistic in the present-day situation of global capitalism. Dismantling of the harmonious social fabric of the past and its replacement by commercialized transactions fetching high returns on financial assets subject to risks under uncertainty, seem to be the pattern of the future. This of course goes hand-in-hand with hardships faced by the underprivileged masses having no opportunity for a change.

In a similar tone, it has also been held that the notion of the 'modern state' has no space for decent survival of human beings.[56] Instead, elites commanding the power to dictate policies internalize the colonial connections of the past by distancing the state and the society, leaving far behind the idea of a developmental state.

The rise of finance under contemporary capitalism, as discussed in the previous chapters relating to the EMEs, has thus relied on a multipronged approach, combining its quantitative expanse in the economy to socio-political structures which simultaneously initiate and sustain the power of finance. The process carries on, generating financial wealth for a privileged few while deprivation for the majority continues unabated. Better days for those who are currently deprived have to wait for an aggressive plan of political change which will enable the real economy to prosper, and with an agenda of fair distribution. This in turn needs to initiate a transformation in the current role of finance and make it a socially relevant activity which contributes to expansion as well as equality in the real economy. This can only be achieved by having a proactive and democratic political set-up.

Notes

1 See, for details, Sen (1992) and Sen (2023a).
2 Gramsci (1978 [1926]); see also Gramsci (1971).
3 https://www.marxists.org/history/erol/ncm-7/tr-gramsci.htm
4 Fontana (2008).
5 Storm (2018).
6 McKinnon (1973); Shaw (1973).
7 Hayek (2013), p. 69.
8 Storm (2018), p. 201.
9 Epstein (2018).
10 See Sen (2000b).
11 See, for example, Bonizzi, Kaltenbrunner and Powell (2020). Also see, Kvangraven, Koddenbrock and Sylla (2020a); Kvangraven, Koddenbrock and Sylla (2020b); and Koddenbrock, Kvangraven and Sylla (2022).
12 Epstein (2018).
13 Storm (2018).
14 Kalaitzake (2014).
15 Freeman (2014); see also Kalaitzake (2015).
16 Kalaitzake (2015).
17 Ibid.
18 Ibid.
19 Ibid.
20 Epstein (2024).
21 Crotty (2011), p. 4.
22 Epstein and Montecino (2016).
23 Kalaitzake (2014).
24 Sen and Dasgupta (2018).
25 Karwowski and Stockhammer (2017).
26 Kalaitzake (2014).
27 Epstein (2024), Kindle book location (L) 1986–2041.
28 Ibid.
29 Ibid.
30 Crotty (2011).
31 Lapavitsas *et al.* (2010), pp. 21–22.
32 Bagchi (2013).
33 Wray (2008); Sen (2010), pp. 143–63.
34 Baker and McArthur (2009).

[35] Bagchi and Dymski (2007), pp. 172–94.
[36] Bagchi (2013).
[37] Crotty (2011).
[38] Storm (2018).
[39] Epstein (2005).
[40] Storm (2018).
[41] Pozsar and Singh (2011), p. 5.
[42] Epstein (2018).
[43] Mader, Mertens and Zwan, eds (2020).
[44] Storm (2018).
[45] Epstein (2018).
[46] Ibid. See also Sen and Dasgupta (2018).
[47] Epstein (2024).
[48] Ibid.
[49] Achen and Bartels (2016).
[50] Dore (2000).
[51] Bankstone (2022).
[52] Bhandari and Yasunobu (2009).
[53] Polanyi (1944).
[54] Ibid.
[55] Ibid.
[56] Nandy (2003).

References

Achen, C.H. and L.M. Bartels (2016), *Democracy for Realists: Why Elections Do Not Produce Responsive Government*, Princeton: Princeton University Press.

Aguila, E., A. Akhmedjonov, R. Basurto-Davila, K.B. Kumar, S. Kups and H. Shatz (2012), *United States and Mexico: Ties That Bind, Issues That Divide*, California: Rand Corporation.

Aizenman, J. (2013), 'The Impossible Trinity: From Policy Trilemma to Policy Quadrilemma', *Global Journal of Economics*, vol. 2, no. 1, pp. 1–17.

Aizenman, J. and J. Lee (2007), 'International Reserves, Precautionary vs Mercantilist Views: Theory and Evidence', *Open Economics Review*, vol. 18, pp. 191–214.

Agence France-Presse (AFP) (2014), 'Argentina in 2001: The Biggest Default in History', AFP, 29 July, available at https://sg.finance.yahoo.com/news/argentina-2001-biggest-default-history-183426906.html.

Amadeo, K. (2022), 'What is Petro-Dollar?', available at https://www.thebalancemoney.com/what-is-a-petrodollar-3306358

Baer, W. (1976), 'The Brazilian Miracle: The Issues and the Literature', *Bulletin of the Society for Latin American Studies*, Society for Latin American Studies, no. 24, March, pp. 3–22.

Bagchi, A.K. (2011), *Perilous Passage: Mankind and the Global Ascendancy of Capital*, Delhi: Oxford University Press.

———— (2013), 'Lunging towards Corporate Feudalism', in S. Sen and A. Chakrabarti, eds, *Development on Trial*, Delhi: Orient BlackSwan, pp. 3–28.

Bagchi, A.K. and G.A. Dymski, eds (2007), *Capture and Exclude: Developing Economies and the Poor in Global Finance*, Delhi: Tulika Books.

Baker, D. and T. McArthur (2009), 'The Value of the "Too Big to Fail" Big Bank Subsidy', Centre for Economic Policy Research (CEPR), available at https://www.researchgate.net/profile/Dean-Baker-2/publication/46465053_The_Value_of_the_Too_Big_to_Fail_Big_Bank_Subsidy/links/543bcaa60cf204cab1db3210/The-Value-of-the-aToo-Big-to-Faila-Big-Bank-Subsidy.pdf.

Ball, C.P. and J.A. Reyes (2004), 'Inflation Targeting or Fear of Floating', *International Journal of Finance and Economics*, January.

Bankstone, C.L. (2022), *Rethinking Social Capital*, Cheltenham and Northampton, MA: Edward Elgar.

Basotti, P. (2022), *Setbacks and Advances in the Modern Latin American Economy*, New York and Abingdon, Oxon: Routledge.

Bateman, B.W. (1991), 'The Rules of the Road: Keynes's Theoretical Rationale for Public Policy', in B.W. Bateman and J.B. Davis, eds, *Keynes and Philosophy: Essays on the Origin of Keynes's Thought*, Cheltenham: Edward Elgar.

Bernanke, B.S. (2020), 'The New Tools of Monetary Policy', *American Economic Review*, vol. 110, no. 4, April, pp. 943–83.

Bhandari, H. and K. Yasunobu (2009), 'What is Social Capital? A Comprehensive Review of the Concept', *Asian Journal of Social Science*, vol. 37, no. 3, pp. 480–510.

Bonizzi, B., A. Kaltenbrunner and J. Powell (2020), 'Subordinate Financialization in Emerging Capitalist Countries', in P. Mader, D. Mertens and N. van der Zwan, eds, *The Routledge International Handbook of Financialization*, London: Routledge, pp. 177–87.

Bose, S. and A. Kumar (2018), 'Financialization in Contemporary Capitalism: An Inter-Sectoral Approach to Trace Source of Instability in Finance, Real Estate and Business Services in India', in S. Sen and C. Marcuzzo, eds, *The Changing Face of Imperialism: Colonialism to Contemporary Capitalism*, Abingdon, Oxon and New York: Routledge, pp. 267–94.

Branford, S. and B. Kucinski (1988), *The Debt Squads: The U.S., the Banks, and Latin America*, London and New Jersey: Zed Books.

Brandolini, S.M. Dall'Aste and R. Scazzieri, eds (2011), *Fundamental Uncertainty: Rationality and Plausible Reasoning*, Palgrave Macmillan.

Braudel, F. (1977), *Afterthoughts on Material Civilization and Capitalism*, Baltimore and London: Johns Hopkins University Press.

Brazil Stock Market (BOVESPA) (1988–2023), Historical Data, https://tradingeconomics.com/

_____ (2024), Forecast, https://tradingeconomics.com/.

Bukowski, E., S. Xu, Z. Liu and N. Crukhorn (2024), 'China's 2024 Third Plenum: 6 Key Takeaways', 29 July, available at https://apco worldwide.com/blog/chinas-2024-third-plenum-six-key-takeaways/

Cardinale, I. (2020), 'Towards a Structural Political Economy of Resources', in M. Baranzini, F. Rotondi and R. Scazzieri, eds, *Resources, Production and Structural Dynamics*, Cambridge: Cambridge University Press, pp. 198–210.

Cardinale, I., J. Galbraith and R. Scazzieri (2024), 'Structural Dynamics and the Wealth of Nations: Luigi Pasinetti's System of Economic Theory', *Structural Change and Economic Dynamics*, vol. 69, pp. 692–98.

Chakrabarti, A., A.K. Dhar and B. Dasgupta (2015), *The Indian Economy in Transition: Globalization, Capitalism and Development*, Delhi: Cambridge University Press.

Chandrasekhar, C.P. and J. Ghosh (2002), *The Market That Failed: A Decade of Neoliberal Economic Reforms*, Delhi: Leftword Books.

Chang, Ha-Joon (2002), 'Kicking Away the Ladder: An Unofficial History of Capitalism, Especially in Britain and the United States', *Challenge*, vol. 45, no. 5, pp. 63–95.

Cibils, A. and C. Allami (2013), 'Financialization vs Development Finance: The Case of the Post-Crisis Argentine Banking System', *Revue de la Regulation*, vol. 13.

Coy, P. (2023), 'The Scientist Who Foresaw China's Stagnation', *New York Times*, 28 August, available at https://www.nytimes.com/2023/08/28/opinion/chinese-economy-yi-fuxian.html.

Crotty, J. (2009), 'Structural Causes of the Global Financial Crisis: A Critical Assessment of the New Financial Architecture', *Cambridge Journal of Economics*, vol. 33, no. 4, July, pp. 563–80.

_____ (2011), 'The Bonus-Driven "Rainmaker" Financial Firm: How These Firms Enrich Top Employees, Destroy Shareholder Value and Create Systemic Financial Instability', Political Economy Research Institute (PERI) Working Paper, University of Massachusetts, Amherst, June.

_____ (2013), 'Realism of Assumptions Does Matter: Why Keynes–Minsky Theory Must Replace Efficient Market Theory as a Guide to Financial Regulation Policy', in M. Wolfson and G. Epstein, eds, *Political Economy of Financial Crises*, New York: Oxford University Press, pp. 133–58.

Darity Jr, W.A. (1985), 'Loan Pushing: Doctrine and Theory', *International Finance Discussion Papers*, no. 253, available at https://www.federalreserve.gov/pubs/ifdp/1985/253/ifdp253.pdf.

Dasgupta, Z. and S. Raghavendra (2024), 'On the Fall of Household Savings', *The Hindu*, 22 April.

David, D. (1955), 'Different Views on Uncertainty and Some Policy Implications', in P. Davidson and J. Kregel, eds, *Improving the Global Economy*, Cheltenham: Edward Elgar.

Davidson, P. (2003), 'The Terminology of Uncertainty in Economics and the Philosophy of an Active Role of Government Policies', in J. Runde and S. Mizuhara, eds, *The Philosophy of Keynes's Economics: Probability, Uncertainty and Convention*, Abingdon, Oxon: Routledge, pp. 230–31.

de Carvalho, F.C.C. (1988), 'Keynes on Probability, Uncertainty and Decision Making', *Journal of Post Keynesian Economics*, vol. 11, no. 1, pp. 66–81.

de Carvalho, F.C.C. and F.E.P. de Souza (2010), 'Financial Regulation and Macroeconomic Stability in Brazil in the Aftermath of the Russian Crisis', available at http://www.itf.org.ar/pdf/documentos/65-2010.pdf.

Dhar, B. (2025), 'Trump's America First Trade Policy Puts India at Distinct Disadvantage', available at https://thefederal.com/category/opinion/trumps-america-first-trade-policy-puts-india-at-distinct-disadvantage-172476.

Dodd, R. and S. Griffith-Jones (2007), 'Brazil's Derivatives Markets: Hedging, Central Bank Intervention and Regulation', United Nations Economic Commission for Latin America and the Caribbean (CEPAL – Comisión Económica para América Latina y el Caribe), repositorio.cepal.org.

Dore, R. (2000), *Stock Market Capitalism: Welfare Capitalism: Japan and Germany versus the Anglo-Saxons*, New York: Oxford University Press.

Dow, S. (2016), 'Uncertainty: A Diagrammatic Treatment', *Economics* (e-journal), vol. 10, no. 1, pp. 1–25.

Dow, S., J. Jespersen and G. Tily, eds (2018), *Money, Method and Contemporary Post-Keynesian Economics*, Cheltenham and Northampton, MA: Edward Elgar.

Dunn, S. (2001), 'Bounded Rationality Is Not Fundamental Uncertainty:

A Post-Keynesian Perspective', *Journal of Post-Keynesian Economics*, vol. 23, no. 4, pp. 567–87.

———— (2008), *Uncertain Foundations of Post-Keynesian Economics: Essays in Explorations*, Abingdon, Oxon: Routledge.

Durand, C. (2007), *Fictitious Capital: How Finance is Appropriating Our Future*, London and New York: Verso, pp. 27–56.

Dymski, G., G. Epstein and R. Pollin (2016), *Transforming the U.S. Financial System: An Equitable and Efficient Structure for the 21st Century*, New York: Routledge.

Echenique-Romero, X. (2021), 'Excess International Liquidity and Corporate Financing in Mexico: Reflections from USA Monetary Policy of Quantitative Easing', in N. Levy-Orlik, J.A. Bustamante-Torres and L-P Rochon, eds, *Capital Movements and Corporate Dominance in Latin America: Reduced Growth and Increased Instability*, Cheltenham and Northampton, MA: Edward Elgar, pp. 140–57.

Epstein, G. (2018), 'On the Social Efficiency of Finance', *Development and Change*, vol. 49, no. 2, pp. 330–52.

———— (2021), 'Financialization: There's Something Happening Here', in V. Upadhyay and P. Singh, eds, *Global Political Economy: A Critique of Contemporary Capitalism*, London: Routledge.

Epstein, G., ed. (2005), *Financialization and the World Economy*, Chelten-ham and Northampton, MA: Edward Elgar.

———— (2024), *Busting the Bankers' Club: Finance for the Rest of Us*, Oakland, CA: University of California Press, Kindle edition, Location (L) 2389–93.

Epstein, G. and J.A. Montecino (2016), 'Overcharged: The High Cost of High Finance', The Roosevelt Institute, 12 July.

Fitzgerald, M. and J. Gallup, eds (2023), *The Guide to Restructuring*, Latin Lawyer, https://latinlawyer.com/guide/the-guide-restructuring/third-edition/article/lessons-argentinas-default-its-international-sovereign-debt, accessed 20 October 2024

Fleming, J.M. (1962), 'Domestic Financial Policies under Fixed and under Floating Exchange Rates', IMF Staff Papers, vol. 9, Washington D.C.: International Monetary Fund, November, pp. 369–79.

Fontana, B. (2008), 'Hegemony and Power in Gramsci', in R. Howson and K. Smith, eds, *Hegemony*, New York: Routledge.

Freeman, A. (2014), 'The Future of Capitalism Without Owners', in R. O'Brien, ed., *Finance and the International Economy 8: The AMEX*

Bank Review Prize Essays: In Memory of Robert Marjolin, New York: Oxford University Press.

Galbraith, J.K. (2010), 'The Great Crisis and the American Response', Public Policy Brief No. 112, Levy Economics Institute of Bard College, Annandale-on-Hudson, NY.

Gallagher, K., J.A. Ocampo, M. Zhang and Y. Yongding, eds (2014), *Capital Account Liberalization in China: The Need for a Balanced Approach*, Boston, MA: Pardee Centre, Boston University.

Ghosh, J. (2022), *The Making of a Catastrophe: The Disastrous Economic Fallout of the Covid-19 Pandemic in India*, Delhi: Aleph Book Company.

Giovannini, M. (2020), 'China Plans to Turn its Lenders into Universal Banks', available at https://news.cgtn.com/news/2020-07-05/China-plans-to-turn-its-lenders-into-universal-banks-RRikfses0w/index.html.

Gottschalk, R. and S. Sen (2010), 'Prudential Norms for the Financial Sector: Is Development a Missing Dimension? The Cases of Brazil and India', in R. Gottschalk, ed., *The Basel Capital Accords in Developing Countries: Challenges for Development Finance*, London: Palgrave Macmillan, pp.16–33.

Government of India (GoI) (2025), *Economic Survey of India 2024–25*, Delhi: Ministry of Finance, Government of India.

Gramsci, A. (1971), *Selections from the Prison Notebooks of Antonio Gramsci*, New York: International Publishers.

———— ([1926] 1978), 'Some Aspects of the Southern Question' (unfinished text), in Quintin Hoare, trans. and ed., *Antonio Gramsci: Selections from Political Writings (1921–1926)*, London: Lawrence and Wishart, available at https://cpb-us-e1.wpmucdn.com/blogs.uoregon.edu/dist/f/6855/files/2014/03/gramsci-southern-question1926-2jf8c5x.pdf.

Griffith-Jones, S., J.A. Ocampo and J.E. Stiglitz, eds (2010), *Time for a Visible Hand: Lessons from the 2008 World Financial Crisis*, New York: Oxford University Press.

Gros, D. (2023), 'The Real Problem With China's Economy', *Project Syndicate*, 11 September, available at https://www.project-syndicate.org/commentary/china-slowing-growth-excess-savings-declining-investment-by-daniel-gros-2023-09.

Harris, L. (1988), 'Alternative Perspectives on the Financial System', in L. Harris and Jet Coakley, eds, *New Perspectives on the Financial System*, London: Croom Helm.

Hayek, F.A. (2013), 'The Market and Other Orders', in *The Collected Works of F.A Hayek*, vol. 15, edited by Bruce Caldwell, Chicago: University of Chicago Press.

He, L. (2023), 'China's Economy Regains Momentum, But Real Estate Remains a Drag', *CNN*, 18 October, available at https://edition.cnn.com/2023/10/17/economy/china-q3-gdp-intl-hnk/.

Hirai, T., M.C. Marcuzzo and P. Mehrling, eds (2013), *Keynesian Reflections*, Delhi: Oxford University Press.

International Monetary Fund (IMF), *International Financial Statistics*, various years.

_____ (2024), *World Economic Outlook Database*, October.

Jin, K. (2023), *The New China Playbook: Beyond Socialism and Capitalism*, New York: Viking, Penguin Random House.

Kalaitzake, M. (2014), 'Politics, Power and Contemporary Financialization', Working Paper, University College, Dublin, July.

_____ (2015), 'Political Capture by the Financial Industry', in N. Buxton and M.B. Dumontier, eds, *State of Power: An Annual Anthology of Global Power and Resistance*, Amsterdam: The Transnational Institute, pp. 17–27, available at https://www.tni.org/files/download/tni_state-of-power-2015.pdf.

Kaltenbruner, A. and Painceira, J.P. (2018), 'Subordinated Financial Integration and Financialization in Emerging Capitalist Economies: The Brazilian Experience', *New Political Economy*, vol. 23, no. 3, pp. 290–313.

Karwowski, E. (2020), 'Economic Development and Variegated Financialization in Emerging Economies', in P. Mader, D. Mertens and N. van der Zwan, eds, *The Routledge International Handbook of Financialization*, Routledge, pp. 162–76.

Karwowski, E. and E. Stockhammer (2017), 'Financialization in Emerging Market Economies: A Systematic Overview and Comparison with Anglo-Saxon Economies', *Economic and Political Studies*, vol. 5, no. 1, pp. 60–86, https://doi.org/10.1080/20954816.2016.1274520.

Keynes, J.M. (1921), *A Treatise on Probability*, London: Macmillan & Co.

_____ (1936), *The General Theory of Employment, Interest and Money*, Harcourt, Brace & Co.

_____ (1937), 'The General Theory of Employment', *Quarterly Journal of Economics*, vol. 51, no. 2, pp. 209–23.

_____ , *The Papers of John Maynard Keynes*, Archive Centre, King's College, Cambridge, TP/D/6.

Koddenbrock, K., I.H. Kvangraven and N.S. Sylla (2022), 'Beyond Financialization: The Longue Durée of Finance and Production in the Global South', *Cambridge Journal of Economics*, vol. 46, no. 4, July, pp. 703–33.

Kumar, A. (2021), 'Rising National Income but Declining Welfare of People', *Leaflet*, 17 March, available at https://theleaflet.in/rising-national-income-but-declining-welfare-of-people/.

Kvangraven, I.H., K. Koddenbrock and N.S. Sylla (2020a), 'Beyond the Stereotype: Restating the Relevance of the Dependency Research Programme', *Development and Change*, 4 June.

_____ (2020b), 'Financial Subordination and Uneven Financialization in 21st Century Africa', *Community Development Journal*, vol. 56, no. 1, October, pp. 119–40.

Lapavistas, C. (2013), *Profiiting without Producing: How Finance Exploits Us All*, New York: Verso.

Lapavitsas, C., J. Powell, A. Kaltenbrunner, D. Lindo, J. Michell, J.P. Painceira, E. Pires, A. Stenfors and N. Teles (2010), 'Eurozone Crisis: Beggar Thyself and Thy Neighbour', *Journal of Balkan and Near Eastern Studies*, vol. 12, no. 4, pp. 321–73.

Leonardo, F. (2018), *Sovereign Debt Crisis and Negotiations in Brazil and Mexico*, New York: Palgrave Macmillan.

Levy-Orlik, N. and J.A. Bustamante-Torres (2021), 'The Unique Development of Non-financial Corporations in Latin America', in N. Levy-Orlik, J.A. Bustamante-Torres and L-P Rochon, eds, *Capital Movements and Corporate Dominance in Latin America: Reduced Growth and Increased Instability*, Cheltenham and Northampton, MA: Edward Elgar, pp. 89–105.

Levy-Orlik, N. and J.A. Bustamante-Torres, eds (2020), *Financialization in Latin America: Challenges of the Export-Led Growth Model*, Abingdon, Oxon: Routledge.

López, J., A. Sanchez and A. Spanos (2011), 'Macroeconomic Linkages in Mexico', *Metroeconomica*, vol. 62, no. 2, pp. 356–85.

Lubin, D. (2022), 'Why a More Inward-Looking China Is Bad News for the World', available at https://www.chathamhouse.org/2022/10/why-more-inward-looking-china-bad-news-world-economy.

Lucio, F.G.C., R.A. de Castro Pereira and J.W.F. Gomes (2020), 'Grease or Sand the Wheels? A State-Level Approach on Corruption in Brazil', *Theoretical Economics Letters*, vol. 10, no. 3, June.

Mader, P., D. Mertens and N. van der Zwan, eds (2020), *The Routledge International Handbook of Financialization*, Abingdon, Oxon: Routledge.

Mani, S. (2012), 'Have China and India Become More Innovative Since the Onset of Reforms?', in A. Bagchi and A. D'Costa, eds, *Transformation and Development: The Political Economy of Transition in India and China*, Delhi: Oxford University Press, pp. 273–300.

Marx, K. (2016), *Capital (Das Kapital)*, vols 1, 2, 3, Delhi: Fingerprint! Publishing.

McKinnon, R. (1973), *Money and Capital in Economics*, Washington, D.C.: Brookings Institution.

Mundell, R.A. (1960), 'The Monetary Dynamics of International Adjustment under Fixed and Flexible Exchange Rates', *Quarterly Journal of Economics*, 74, no. 2, pp. 227–57.

Nandy, A. (2003), *The Romance of the State: And the Fate of Dissent in the Tropics*, Delhi: Oxford University Press.

Napolitano, M. (2018), 'The Brazilian Military Regime: 1964–85', in *Oxford Research Encyclopedia of Latin American History*, 26 April, https://doi.org/10.1093/acrefore/9780199366439.013.413.

Nesvetailova, A. (2010), *Financial Alchemy in Crisis: The Great Liquidity Illusion*, London: Pluto Press.

Nolan, P. (2012), *Is China Buying the World?*, Cambridge, UK and Malden, MA: Polity Press.

O'Donnell, R. (1990), 'Keynes's Weight of Argument and Its Bearing on Rationality and Uncertainty', in B.W. Bateman and J.B. Davis Keynes, eds, *Philosophy: Essays on the Origin of Keynes's Thought*, Cheltenham: Edward Elgar.

Oliveira, G. and I.D. Müller (2021), 'Economic History, Developmentalism, and Neoliberalism in Contemporary Brazil', in P.A. Baisotti, ed., *Setbacks and Advances in Latin American Economies*, New York: Routledge.

Palley, T.I. (2012), *From Financial Crisis to Stagnation: The Destruction of Shared Prosperity and the Role of Economics*, New York: Cambridge University Press.

Pasinetti, L.L. (1963), *Structural Economic Dynamics: A Theory of the Economic Consequences of Human Learning*, Cambridge: Cambridge University Press.

———— (1981), *Structural Change and Economic Growth: A Theoretical Essay on the Dynamics of the Wealth of Nations*, Cambridge: Cambridge University Press.

Patnaik, U. and P. Prabhat (2016), *A Theory of Imperialism*, Delhi: Tulika Books and New York: Columbia University Press.

People's Bank of China (2012), *Survey and Statistics Reports*, Financial Survey and Statistics Department, 13 February and 17 April.

Polanyi, K. (1944), *The Great Transformation: The Political and Economic Origins of Our Time*, Boston, MA: Beacon Press.

Pozsar, Z. and M. Singh (2011), *The Nonbank–Bank Nexus and the Shadow Banking System*, International Monetary Fund.

Rajan, R. (2017), *I Do What I Do*, Gurugram: HarperCollins India.

Rapoport, M. and N. Brenta (2021), 'The Argentine Foreign Debt', in P.A. Baisotti, ed., *Setbacks and Advances in Latin American Eco-nomies*, New York: Routledge.

Reserve Bank of India (RBI) (1985), *Report of the Committee to Review the Working of the Monetary System* (Chairman: Sukhamoy Chakravarty), RBI.

———— (2008), *Report of the Committee on Financial Inclusion* (Chairman: C. Rangarajan), RBI.

———— (2014), *Report of the Expert Committee to Revise and Strengthen the Monetary Policy Framework* (Chairman: Urjit Patel), RBI.

———— (1990–2024), *Handbook of Statistics on Indian Economy*, RBI.

————, *Database on the Indian Economy*, various years.

Roberts, J.M. (2011), 'Holding the Kirchners Accountable for Argentina's Economic Freefall', *Backgrounder*, no. 2527, The Heritage Foundation, 4 March, available at https://www.heritage.org/americas/report/holding-the-kirchners-accountable-argentinas-economic-freefall, accessed 20 October 2024.

Robinson, J. (1974), 'Contribution of Keynes to Economic Theory', in *The Papers of Professor Joan Violet Robinson*, JVR/iii/3/13.1/1, King's College, Cambridge.

———— (1979), *Aspects of Development and Underdevelopment*, Cambridge: Cambridge University Press.

Rosario, J.D. (2023), 'Inside IMF, Stance Hardens on Argentina as $44 bln Deal Skids off Track', 9 November, available at https://www.reuters.com/markets/inside-imf-stance-hardens-argentina-44-bln-deal-skids-off-track-2023-11-09.

Rosser, J.B. (2001), 'Alternative Keynesian and Post Keynesian Perspective on Uncertainty and Expectations', *Journal of Post Keynesian Economics*, vol. 23, no. 4, pp. 545–66.

Roubini, N. and S. Mihm (2010) *Crisis Economics: A Crash Course in the Future of Finance*, New York: Penguin.

Saith, A. (2022), *Cambridge Economics in the Post Keynesian Era: The Eclipse of Heterodox Traditions*, Palgrave Studies in the History of Economic Thought, Springer International Publishing.

Salama, P. (2018), 'Is the Change in Globalization's Rhythm an Opportunity for Latin America's Emerging Economies?' in P. Chaderevian, ed., *The Political Economy of Lula's Brazil*, Abingdon, Oxon and New York: Routledge, pp. 14–32.

———— (2022), 'Why Do Latin American Countries Suffer from Long-Term Economic Stagnation?', in P.A. Baisotti, ed., *Setbacks and Advances in Latin American Economies*, New York: Routledge, pp. 59–60.

Scazzieri, R. (2022), 'Instability and Structural Dynamics in the Macroeconomy: A Policy Framework', in A. Arnon, M. Cristina Marcuzzo and A. Rosselli, eds, *Financial Markets in Perspective: Lessons from Economic History and History of Economic Thought*, Cham, Switzerland: Springer.

Sen, S. (1992), *Colonies and Empire: India 1870–1914*, Delhi: Orient Longman.

———— (2000a), *Trade and Dependence: Essays on the Indian Economy*, Delhi: Sage.

———— (2000b), 'Tied Loans, the Liquidity Gap and the Two-gap Models of Aid: An Exercise on Indian Data', in S. Sen, *Trade and Dependence: Essays on the Indian Economy*, Delhi: Sage, pp. 86–105.

———— (2003), *Global Finance at Risk*, London: Palgrave.

———— (2007a), *Globalization and Development*, Delhi: National Book Trust.

———— (2007b), 'China in the Bull Shop: Dealing with Finance after WTO', in A. Bagchi and G. Dymski, eds, *Capture and Exclude: Developing Economies and the Poor in Global Finance*, Delhi: Tulika Books, pp. 305–16.

———— (2008), 'Financial Reforms in India', in L. de Paula and P. Arestis, eds, *Financial Liberalization in Emerging Economies*, Basingstoke: Palgrave Macmillan, pp. 173–93.

———— (2010), 'The Meltdown of the Global Economy: A Keynes–

Minsky Episode?', Working Paper no. 623, Levy Economics Institute of Bard College, New York, September.

———— (2012), 'China in the Global Economy: Encountering the Systemic Risks', in A.K. Bagchi and A. D'Costa, eds, *Transformation and Development: The Political Economy of Transition in India and China*, Delhi: Oxford University Press, pp. 199–219.

———— (2013), 'Currency Concerns under Uncertainty', *Economic and Political Weekly*, vol. 48, no. 25, pp. 30–33.

———— (2013a), 'Uncertainty and Speculation in the Keynesian Tradition: Relevance in Commodity Futures', in T. Hirai, M.C. Marcuzzo and P. Mehrling, eds, *Keynesian Reflections*, Delhi: Oxford University Press, pp. 225–43.

———— (2014a), *Dominant Finance and Stagnant Economies*, Delhi: Oxford University Press.

———— (2014b), 'De-regulated Finance in China: A Critical Analysis', in K. Gallagher, J.A. Ocampo, M. Zhang and Y. Yongding, eds, *Capital Account Liberalization in China: The Need for a Balanced Approach*, Boston: Pardee Centre, Boston University, pp. 109–19.

———— (2015a), 'Turbulence and Stability in Financial Markets: China in Recent Times', *Third World Resurgence*, no. 300, August, pp. 22–24.

———— (2015b), 'The Indian Economy under Economic Reforms: Responses from the Society and the State', in T. Hirai, ed., *Capitalism and the World Economy: The Light and Shadow of Globalization*, London: Routledge, pp. 219–33.

———— (2019), 'Official Reforms and the Real Economy', *Economic and Political Weekly*, vol. 54, no. 38, September.

———— (2020) 'Investment Decisions under Uncertainty', *Journal of Post Keynesian Economics*, vol. 43, no. 2, pp. 267–280, doi:10.1080/01603477.2019.1571927.

———— (2021a), 'Financial Boom at a Time of Economic Stagnation', *The Hindu*, 18 January, available at https://www.thehindu.com/opinion/lead/financial-boom-at-a-time-of-economic-stagnation/article33595248.ece.

———— (2021b), 'De-regulation of Finance in China and India: A Post-Keynesian Analysis', in B. Bonizzi, A. Kaltenbrunner and R.A. Ramos, eds, *Emerging Economies and the Global Financial System*, London: Routledge, pp. 258–74.

———— (2023a), 'Could Britain Continue with the Gold Standard in

Absence of Colonial India?', *Review of Political Economy*, vol. 35, no. 2, pp. 407–20.

_____ (2023b), 'Patterns of Structural Dynamics at Different Stages of Capitalism: USA and India', *Structural Change and Economic Dynamics*, vol. 65, pp. 468–73.

_____ (2024), 'Book Review of *Capital Movements and Corporate Dominance over Latin America: Reduced Growth and Increased Instability*, edited by N. Levy-Orlik, J. Alonso Bustamante-Torres, L-P Rochon', *Review of Political Economy*, vol. 36, no. 1, pp. 385–88.

_____ (2025), 'How Tariff Wars Lead to the Subordination of Developing Countries', 31 March, available at https://www.networkideas. org/news-analysis/2025/03/tariff-wars/.

Sen, S., ed. (1996), *Financial Fragility, Debt and Economic Reforms*, London: Macmillan.

Sen, S. and Z. Dasgupta (2014), 'Economic Policies in India: For Economic Stimulus, or for Austerity and Volatility?', *PSL Quarterly Review*, vol. 67, no. 271, pp. 423–50.

_____ (2018), 'Financialization and Corporate Investments: The Indian Case', *Review of Keynesian Economics*, vol. 6, no. 1, January.

_____ (2023), 'India follows the neo-liberal monetary norms: contracting the space for financial inclusion in her economy', *Monetary Policy Institute Blog*, https://medium.com/@monetarypolicyinstitute/india-follows-the-neo-liberal-monetary-norms-contracting-the-space-for-financial-inclusion-in-her-a44df47b60f2.

Sen, S. and S.K. Ghosh (2005), 'Basel Norms, Indian Banking Sector and Impact on Credit to SMEs and the Poor', *Economic and Political Weekly*, vol. 40, no. 12, pp. 1167–80.

Sen, S. and M. Pal (2010), 'Trading in India's Commodity Future Markets', Working Paper no. 2010/03, Institute of Studies in Industrial Development (ISID), Delhi.

Sen, S. and C. Marcuzzo, eds (2018), *The Changing Face of Imperialism: From Colonialism to Contemporary Capitalism*, Routledge.

Sen, K. and R.R. Vaidya (1997), *The Process of Financial Liberalization in India*, Delhi: Oxford University Press.

_____ (2014), *Dominant Finance and Stagnant Economies*, Delhi: Oxford University Press.

Shaw, E. (1973), *Financial Deepening in Economic Development*, New York: Oxford University Press.

Silver, C. (2022), 'The U.S. Labels China a Currency Manipulator', available at https://www.investopedia.com/the-u-s-treasury-officially-labels-china-a-currency-manipulator-4766799.

Simon, H.A. (1987), 'Bounded Rationality', in J. Eatwell, M. Milgate and P. Newman, eds, *The New Palgrave Dictionary of Economics*, London: Macmillan.

Singer, H.W. (1996), 'Alternate Approaches to Adjustment and Stabilization', in S. Sen, ed., *Financial Fragility, Debt and Economic Reforms*, London: Macmillan.

Sriram, M.S., ed. (2018), *Talking Financial Inclusion in Liberalized India: Conversations with Governors of Reserve Bank of India*, Abingdon, Oxon and New York: Routledge.

Stanley, L. (2018), *Emerging Market Economies and Financial Globalization: Argentina, Brazil, China, India and South Korea*, London: Anthem Press.

Stockhammer, E. (2004), 'Financialization and the Slowdown of Accumulation', *Cambridge Journal of Economics*, vol. 28, no. 5, pp. 719–41.

Storm, S. (2018), 'A Debate on the Social Efficiency of Modern Finance', *Development and Change*, International Institute of Social Studies, vol. 49, no. 2, pp. 302–29.

Swanson, A. (2019), 'The U.S. Labeled China a Currency Manipulator', available at https://www.nytimes.com/2019/08/06/business/economy/china-currency-manipulator.html.

Sweney, M. (2023), 'Package of Spending Cuts Introduced in Attempt to Tackle Country's Worst Economic Crisis in Decades', available at https://www.theguardian.com/world/2023/dec/13/.

Tran, H. (2024), 'Key Takeaways from China's Third Plenum 2024', 23 July, available at https://www.atlanticcouncil.org/blogs/econographics/key-takeaways-from-chinas-third-plenum-2024/.

United Nations Conference on Trade and Development (UNCTAD) (2022), *Trade and Development Report*.

Wani, S. (2025), 'Agricultural Protectionism Pushes up India's Import Tariff', *The Hindu*, 19 February.

Watkins, Thayer, 'Jose Sarney, Hyperinflation and the Cruzado Plan in Brazil in the Late 1980s', https://www.sjsu.edu/faculty/watkins/cruzado.htm.

Wray, R. (2008), 'Financial Markets Meltdown: What Can We Learn from Minsky?', Public Policy Brief No. 94, Levy Economics Institute of Bard College, NY, available at www.levyinstitute.org.publications

Yao, K. (2020), 'What We Know About China's "Dual Circulation"

Economic Strategy', 9 September, available at https://www.reuters.com/article/world/asia-pacific/what-we-know-about-chinas-dual-circulation-economic-strategy-idUSKBN2600B4/.

Yongding, Y. (2012), 'Rebalancing the Chinese Economy', *Oxford Review of Economic Policy*, vol. 28, no. 3, pp. 551–68.

———— (2019), 'The Next Phase of Trump's Trade War with China', 6 July, available at https://www.chinausfocus.com/finance-economy/the-next-phase-of-trumps-trade-war-with-china.

———— (2023a), 'The Road Back to Growth in China', *Project Syndicate*, 9 May, available at https://www.project-syndicate.org/commentary/state-infrastructure-investment-would-fight-deflation-boost-growth-in-china-by-yu-yongding-2023-05.

———— (2023b), 'China's Response to Decoupling', *Project Syndicate*, 28 June, available at https://www.project-syndicate.org/commentary/economic-decoupling-impossible-for-china-and-costly-for-the-west-by-yu-yongding-2023-06.

——— (2023c), 'China's Policy-Induced Slowdown', *Project Syndicate*, 4 October, available at https://www.project-syndicate.org/commentary/china-growth-slowdown-reversible-monetary-fiscal-expansion-by-yu-yongding-2023-10.

——— (2023d) 'Fixing China's Real-Estate Sector', *Project Syndicate*, 30 November, available at https://www.project-syndicate.org/commentary/china-government-deal-with-real-estate-developers-debt-defaults-by-yu-yongding-2023-11.

———— (2024a), 'China's Economic Prospects are Brighter than they Appear', 31 January, available at https://www.scmp.com/comment/opinion/article/3250389/chinas-economic-prospects-are-brighter-they-appear.

———— (2024b), 'China's Economic Fight Against the Coronavirus', *Project Syndicate*, 13 February, available at https://www.project-syndicate.org/commentary/china-economy-three-ways-to-limit-coronavirus-impact-by-yu-yongding-2020-02.

Zhang, M. (2014), 'Should China Accelerate Capital Account Liberalization Now?' in K. Gallagher, J.A. Ocampo, Ming Zhang and Yu Yongding, eds, *Capital Account Liberalization in China: The Need for a Balanced Approach*, Boston: Boston University, pp. 77–87.